No Medal for Second Place:

How to Finish First in Job Interviews

Tom Payne

No Medal for Second Place:

How to Finish First in Job Interviews

Copyright © 2013 Tom Payne

ISBN: 978-1489579089
ISBN-10: 1489579087

EGS Publishing

An imprint of Essential Growth Solutions, LLC

Chicago, IL

CONTENTS

ACKNOWLEDGMENTS

I would like to thank the following employees, volunteers and alumni of the Career Transitions Center of Chicago (CTC): Anita Jenke, the Executive Director, for her work on behalf of jobseekers; Laura Sterkel, the Coaching and Program Director, for her encouragement and support during the final stages of writing and editing this book; Sharon Krohn and Mary Jo Bollero, volunteer coaches at the CTC, for letting me "shadow" them during several of their coaching sessions; Martin Gahbauer, Assistant Director/Employer Relations & Recruiting Coordinator at Loyola University's Career Development Center, for his seminar on informational interviewing. It reminded me what an important tool informational interviewing is, and how most do not know the format that makes this tool effective.

I'd like to thank the staff at the Elam Davies Social Services Center in Chicago: Dan Hula, Director; Jackie Lorens, Associate Program Manager; and Cassandra Price, Case Manager. I'd also like to thank the people they serve. I was asked to give a seminar on interviewing to their clients and I wondered if these executive-level interviewing skills could help those who are battling addiction, inadequate housing and insurance, and other issues. They opened my eyes to the way these techniques can work for anyone, no matter their social status or circumstances.

Finally, I'd like to thank my wife, Joni, for her editorial advice throughout the writing of this work and for continually encouraging me to write this book.

Section One:

The Foundation

1: Running in the Wrong Direction

"It doesn't make sense!"

Julie was talking about her recent job interview. As the memory of it kept replaying in her head it generated more confusion and frustration.

I asked, "What doesn't make sense?"

She continued, "I wasn't hired for a great job opportunity. I know Jane, the person they chose, and her achievements can't compare to mine. Don't they want the best? Isn't that why they conduct interviews?"

Julie found herself in an unfamiliar, uncomfortable place where questions produced more questions and answers could not be found. It led her to do the unthinkable: She turned to someone for help. A close friend referred her to me and today was our first meeting.

I wished my referral came with this warning, "Prepare to have your basic assumptions challenged." Because after giving interviewing seminars for over a decade, coaching many jobseekers both individually and in groups, I've concluded that most of them are running in the wrong direction. This is because they are guided by wrong assumptions.

The Forgotten Relationship: Cause and Effect

I began the process of replacing her wrong assumptions by saying, "What may be confusing you is the way most interviewing processes are designed to find the best-qualified candidates, but the interviewers are not."

"What?"

"Every interviewer *wants* to hire the best candidate, but human nature, the way people are wired, can lead to puzzling decisions. The question we need to answer is, 'What *causes* the interviewer to make his hiring decision?'

"And for the record, I know plenty of women who are hiring authorities, but for simplicity's sake I will stick with masculine pronouns."

Julie said, "Suit yourself. I prefer the feminine."

"Good," I replied. "Now we will have balance." I then continued, "To break the interviewing code, to make sense of your recent interview, we need to think in terms of cause and effect.

"Behind every effect is a cause. The hiring decision is the effect we are trying to cause. So what we're interested in discovering is, 'What causes the hiring decision?'

"Yet, simple as this formula is, not many people know what causes the hiring decision. And that's strange, because if I don't know what these causes are, then how can I purposefully apply them to achieve my goal of being hired? Without this knowledge I am either following an interviewing tradition, based on what seems to work, or my best guesses.

"So Julie, I have an important question for you. Do you know what causes the hiring decision?"

Julie tackled this question with her excellent problem-solving skills. She thought, "The hiring decision is caused by a person's skills and achievements." This thought was followed by a question, "If true, then why was my less-qualified acquaintance hired instead of me?" Although she knew skills and achievements could not be the cause her mind kept coming back to skills and achievements as the answer to my question. She told herself, "Think outside of the box, Julie." But when she kept returning to the same discredited answer she thought, "Think outside of the box? I am the box!"

A Losing Strategy

"Don't worry," I interrupted, as I saw her struggling to find an answer. "I've never had anyone answer that question correctly, because until I ask it, almost no one thinks about it. We'll answer this question in a moment, but first I want to describe the current state of interviewing.

"About fifty years ago one of the greatest defensive football players of his era picked up a fumble, ran sixty-six yards into the end zone and triumphantly threw the football up in the air. There was just one problem. The Minnesota Vikings defensive end, Jim Marshall, had run in the wrong direction and scored for the opposing team. That is the definition of a losing strategy."

"Ouch. How embarrassing."

"As embarrassing as it gets, because running in the wrong direction almost never happens in the NFL. But interviewing is a different game. In this arena almost everyone is running in the wrong direction. This makes for a level playing field until you compete against someone running in the right direction."

Julie said, "When that happens someone who is less qualified can out-interview someone who is more qualified. Am I right?"

I nodded and said, "Yes you are."

She then raised her right hand and said, "Been there. Got the t-shirt. Saw my therapist." Then she passionately added, "And it still makes me mad."

"Yes," I said, "it's painful, because there is no medal for second place in the job-interviewing contest. The Olympics may give out silver and bronze medals, but at the end of an interview the second, third and fourth-place finishers can all expect either a rejection letter or total neglect. This makes the job interview one of life's most unforgiving competitions. It can leave you psychologically bruised."

Julie was slightly emotional when she said, "That's how it felt for me. I'm always confident, always upbeat. But when they chose Jane, it knocked the wind out of me. And it's still shaking my confidence."

"Don't worry. The approach you are going to learn will make you radiate confidence so long as you do the work. And it has been successful under the most extreme conditions. Which brings up a story that should give you hope."

Personally Tested Advice

"At one point I held four jobs during the previous five years. Two times I left jobs for other opportunities. Once I was bankruptcy re-organized out of existence. And one time I was part of a toxic culture that thankfully got rid of me along with many others. But my resume was a disaster.

"One day I heard about a great opportunity. It would involve hiring a national sales team and leading them in the launch of a revolutionary new monitor used during childbirth. I was experienced in medical device sales, but not in obstetrics.

"Unfortunately for me, my bad track record and lack of experience was competing against someone who had twenty years of experience with the world's number one medical-monitoring company. Worse yet, a doctor who authored a textbook on obstetrics used by medical students across the country, and *who worked for the hiring company as a consultant*, recommended him. My competitor was employed and I was not. He worked on the West Coast, where the opportunity was located, and I did not.

"The odds of me being hired were somewhere between far-fetched and absurd. Nonetheless, I got the job."

Julie shook her head, and said, "How did you do it?"

"I ran in the right direction and he didn't."

The Correct, But Unwanted Assumptions

"If we hope to run in the right direction, we need to change our assumptions. Correct assumptions form the foundation of our success and we start laying it by answering the question, 'What causes the hiring-decision-effect?' Once I know this I become a marksman who sees his target and hits it, round after round, while my competitors are firing blindly in all directions. My actions are intentional, and not accidental.

"The answer to this question will also reveal why most people are running in the wrong direction. The correct assumptions are ones we don't want to believe are true. They are distasteful and we tend to reject them out of hand. This makes people cling to the wrong assumption even when the evidence clearly shows it is wrong. Take this assumption."

False Assumption # 1: The Hiring Decision Is Rational

"The hiring decision is, drum roll please, a decision. Decisions are made in the mind. Therefore, the causes of the hiring decision must be psychological in nature.

"Two of the most powerful psychological influences on decision-making are emotion and reason. So Julie, is the hiring authority's decision swayed primarily by rational or emotional forces?"

Julie answered, "The hiring authority analyzes resumes—that's rational. SHE [Julie made sure I caught the change in gender] asks questions to see if we bring special skills to her team and that is rational. After the interview she typically gets together with her team to discuss the various candidates and who would be better. This is an analytical process, so that's rational. I'd have to say emotion may creep into hiring decisions, but it is predominantly rational."

"Whether someone has thought about this question or not, most people interview according to this assumption. They try and give the hiring authority more reasons why they should be hired than their competitors. For example, when asked, 'Tell me about yourself,' they desperately try to pack as many achievements into a five-minute span as possible. Unfortunately, this is running in the wrong direction. It is ineffective, because the hiring decision is more emotional than rational."

Clinging to Wrong Assumptions

Julie shook her head and said, "I'm sorry, but I don't buy that. I just gave you an illustration of how it is a rational process."

"You did. You detailed a standard, rational hiring process. But hiring is not a process, it is a decision made in the mind. And you did not illustrate the hiring authority's psychological state, and whether or not his decision was being influenced by rational or irrational forces.

"I didn't think you would accept the correct assumption, because it is difficult to accept. Who wants to think an important decision, like the hiring decision, is irrational? The idea is offensive. We think, in our attempt to justify ourselves, we are rational creatures. And so we hang onto the wrong assumption even when our own experience shows us it is wrong.

"Can't you see how your recent experience proves my point? When you were passed over for someone less talented, was that a rational decision on the part of the interviewer?"

At that instant Julie knew the strength of her argument was weakened by her own admission. Through gritted teeth she conceded, "No. Like I said, it made no sense."

"Exactly. It was an irrational decision, not a rational one. Somehow Jane made the hiring authority feel more comfortable. Your achievements may be superior to Jane's, but her interviewing approach quieted his fears. And I'm willing to bet her interviewing style made her more likable, while your style hurt your likability."

Julie responded quickly, "What does interviewing style have to do with likability?"

Why Emotion Wins

"Our communication style has everything to do with likability. Let's compare a rational and an emotional communication style and see which one is more likable.

"A guy named Doofus McGrew goes up to Betty Sue with a deadly serious expression on his face and says, 'I have a high I.Q. I am dependable. I've never missed a day at work. I make $150,000 a year. My grandparents and great-grandparents lived to an average age of 90, and my parents are still alive and in perfect health. I find you to be attractive and smart enough for marriage purposes. We are an ideal match. My mother, who is a statistician, has examined the variables and agrees. Will you marry me?'

"Without a moment's hesitation Betty Sue says, 'No.'

"Now let's look at Romeo Jones's approach. He comes up to Betty Sue and seems at ease. He is wearing a big smile and says: 'I may not be the world's authority on what love is, but I do know this: I can't stop thinking about you. And this pleases me, because just thinking about you makes me smile. If you were to accept my marriage proposal you can count on one thing. I will never want to be with anyone else, because my heart doesn't have enough room for another person.'

"Without asking her, 'Will you marry me?' Betty Sue tells Romeo, 'I do.'

"Does the rational or the emotional approach make a person more likable? Doofus's method is very rational, but he fails in his attempt because the rational approach is cold and unfeeling. There is nothing warm about statistics or data-points. Doofus may be a likable guy, but he chose a style that makes him difficult to like. The same is true of an interviewee who intensely delivers a barrage of facts and data about why he is wonderful and a perfect fit for the job. A cold, rational style generates little warmth. It is difficult to like."

The Most Important Decisions and Emotional Influence

"Julie, if you are like most interviewees I bet your approach to the interview is heavy on facts and data. Am I right?"

"Yes, but how else am I going to convince someone I am more than capable of doing the job? You seem to be reducing the interviewing process to a popularity contest, and it has to be so much more."

"It is so much more, because the hiring decision is caused by many emotions, and some are far more powerful than just being likable.

"One of the most counter-intuitive ideas we can have about decision-making is this: The more important the decision, the more powerful the influence of emotions. We naturally think the opposite, because we hate to think of ourselves as irrational, particularly when it comes to making big decisions. But there is a good reason why emotions cause important decisions.

"What makes a decision important are its consequences. If a decision can cause significant pain or gain, then it is important. This decision would be influenced by emotions like the fear of harm and the hope of rewards. Reason would take a back seat. Take, for example, the marriage decision, one of the most important decisions a person can make. It can be a great blessing or a great curse, and no one would dispute the influence emotions exert on this decision.

"The hiring decision can also be a great blessing or curse. You could be a perfect addition to my team, or someone who refuses to fit in and who fights me at every turn.

"Now, you may be the most qualified candidate, but if Jane quieted my fears and you did not, and if she interviewed in a way that made her likable and you did not, then who will I end up hiring? The answer is simple. I hire the less-qualified candidate, because I do not fear hiring her, and because I like her and *want* her on my team."

Julie silently shook her head no. She said, "Reason can always overpower emotion. Sorry, but count me among the people who believe humans are rational."

Even though her experience confirmed the irrationality of the hiring decision she could not bring herself to embrace an assumption that was personally distasteful. So I said, "Few people want to embrace this notion at first, but this illustration sometimes helps them see how reason is weak in the face of emotion.

"Do you have a fear of heights, the dark, snakes, spiders, or any other phobias?"

She shivered a little as she said, "Snakes, spiders and rats. All three of them make me cringe."

"Can I, or anyone else, reason you out of these fears?"

She countered, "But that's a phobia. You can't compare that to a normal decision."

"Okay, is love normal? Have you ever been in love with a person who wasn't right for you? Or have you had a friend in that spot? I've seen the emotion of love nullify reason time after time, making excuse after excuse for their lover's hurtful behavior, until the pain of reality was too great for the person to bear. And this crazy drama affected eminently rational business professionals.

"The power of emotion, and the risk-reward nature of the hiring decision are some of the reasons why this decision is emotionally caused. People hire people they feel comfortable with, who inspire the emotion of trust. And your rational approach to interviewing— bombarding people with facts—does little to inspire the emotions that cause the hiring decision."

Julie's sense of humor made an appearance, "So the bottom line is: Don't be a doofus."

"That pretty much sums it up."

The Vanishing Act

Julie's eyes were starting to open. She thought about how she peppered the hiring authority with 100 reasons why she was the perfect person for the job. She was intense. There was nothing relaxed or warm about her demeanor. She was, in short, not very likable.

She said, "So the cold, unfeeling, rational communication style is difficult to warm up to, and this hurts my interviewing chances. Is that right?"

"Yes" I answered, then added, "but it does even more damage. It makes you disappear."

"What!" Julie exclaimed, her doubt on full display.

"Yes, it makes you disappear," I replied. "If I was a computer I could hear every one of your qualifications, calculate their worth, weigh them on a scale, compare these weighted reasons to those of the other four candidates, and then choose you because your qualifications outweighed theirs. But I'm human and I can't keep up with weighing the information before more arrives. By the third interview all of these facts have blurred together and the candidates all disappear.

"The same thing happened when you went to college. You sat in three one-hour college classes that occurred one after another. How much did you remember?"

"Hardly anything. Like you said, it became a blur."

"That's what happens to the interviewees who use a fact-laden, rational, interviewing style. They become part of the interviewing blur. They disappear in the fog of data.

"Is this starting to make sense?"

"Yes. I may be slow, but I'm not stupid."

"Trust me, I don't underestimate you or your smarts. But now I want to attack another persistent, false assumption. Are you ready to have your mind blown?"

"Again?" Julie asked.

"They say it's therapeutic."

"You enjoy doing this to me, don't you?"

"Yes," I said, because I had the outcome in view.

Lessons

1. Emotions cause important decisions like the hiring decision.

2. Change your direction. Stop presenting endless streams of facts and data. This is a rational approach.

3. We find it difficult to embrace correct assumptions when they seem to reflect poorly on us.

2: The Unwanted Revelation

Julie's defensive body language revealed her understandable discomfort. Like everyone else, she became unsettled when her basic assumptions were upended. But we had to engage in this process, because wrong assumptions are like mental scar tissue. Scar tissue hinders freedom of movement. It does not stretch to accommodate our wishes. If we are to change course and move in the right direction, then we must painfully tear it.

I continued, "I am willing to bet you want absolutely nothing to do with selling, am I right?"

In an instant Julie went from a defensive to a pleading posture, "Please don't tell me I have to sell myself like a salesperson. Please. I can't do it, and I won't."

"Most people, who aren't in sales, feel this way. And I probably agree with you on this subject, but I need to ask a few questions to make sure. What is it you don't like about sales?"

"It's pushy and demanding. It's arrogant. It's obnoxious. I couldn't do it, because it's not me."

"For the record, you are rejecting the traditional sales approach that's associated with selling used cars. I also reject it. It doesn't work in an interview.

"Now, unfortunately, I've got some bad news for you. Julie, you've become a traditional salesperson during interviews."

Julie eyes opened wide and she said, "You can't be serious. There is no way I'm a salesperson!"

False Assumption # 2: I'm Not Selling

I paused for a second and gently continued, "Julie, the wrong assumptions lead everyone to adopt this traditional-sales model. So let's see if what I am saying is true.

"Are you pushy and arrogant? No. Does the traditional-sales model require being this way? No. However, when you dump facts and data on the hiring authority you are acting like a salesperson offering a laundry list of features and benefits. And like a bad salesperson I bet you mostly offer features and fail to illustrate the benefits."

I paused for a moment to let that sink in, then continued, "All interviewees are selling. You, for example, are presenting the product named 'Julie.' The only question is, 'Are you selling yourself effectively or not?' Unfortunately for you, your feature-dumping approach is straight out of a traditional-sales manual, and it doesn't work. You need to use a different model, one that you are completely unfamiliar with.

"What is truly remarkable is the way most interviewing approaches are infected by the traditional-sales model that doesn't work. For example, according to some websites, what is the number one thing most people forget to do during an interview?"

Julie said, "I think I've been to that site. The answer is, 'Ask for the job.' Right?"

"Right. Now this is what is known as 'closing the sale.' This asking for a job is traditional selling at its worst. In traditional sales, the first three rules are, 'Close, close, close.' But that is just the sort of pushy, overly aggressive selling that has no place in most interviews. And it makes no sense.

"Let's say I'm the first person to interview for a job opening and the hiring authority has four other people in line. If I ask for the job what have I accomplished? I force the interviewer to explain to me that he has several other interviews to conduct and cannot make a decision. Now how does that advance my cause?"

"So what should I be doing?"

"You should replace the ineffective model you are currently using with an effective one."

The Effective Interviewing Model

"There are two types of sales: simple and complex. A simple sale involves selling low-cost products or services to one decision-maker. The low cost means there's little risk. If I make a bad buying-decision, then it's no big deal. So fear, or emotion, is not as big a factor in this decision-making process. Close, close, close may work in these situations. This simple-sales approach was the one embraced by the world of interviewing. And it may work for low-wage opportunities.

"Let's say I'm interviewing for a minimum-wage position like washing dishes or something. Here it makes sense to ask for the job. It is doubtful a restaurant will have four interviews lined up for a dishwashing position. There is little fear associated with this hiring decision, so there are very few safeguards to prevent making a bad decision. One person decides. It's a simple sale.

"However, the complex-sales process is very different. The cost of the product or service is higher; therefore, the risks associated with a bad decision are greater. To guard against making a bad decision the buying company puts safeguards in place. There is a team making the buying decision instead of just one person. There are several rounds of sales presentations. This model sounds like it resembles the interviewing process, doesn't it?"

"Yes. Several rounds of interviews with more than one person."

"Right. And in this model a good, complex-salesperson doesn't badger people with silly closing techniques, because he understands the decision will not be made in front of him. The decision-making team typically decides behind closed doors. He also understands that emotions cause the buying decision. So he addresses their fears by showing how his company has minimized the risks involved. He entertains his customers because he wants them to like him. And here is a key point: His many sales presentations do not make the customer feel like they are being sold."[1]

Julie asked, "How is that possible?"

"Part of it has to do with focusing on solutions to the customer's problems. This makes the salesperson seem like he is part of their team, because he is focused on solving their problems, just like they are. But the real secret involves one's communication style.

"We'll get into all of this, but first I want to share a quick story. I was once in charge of a group who sold systems to hospitals that could cost millions of dollars installed. It was a very complex process. And I'll never forget what one decision-maker told me after she visited our corporate headquarters. She said, 'I've been here for two days and you've yet to try and sell me.' And she was telling the truth from her perspective. She was used to the traditional, high-pressure sales approach and our approach was…"

Julie interrupted, "180 degrees different. Did she buy your system?"

"Yes, because customers hate being sold, but they love buying. The same can be said of interviewers. It's one of the reasons why some people begin to dread interviewing. They are constantly being sold, and in a traditional sales way. They don't like it, and every candidate makes them feel uncomfortable until they interview someone who is running in the right direction."

The Danger of Imprecise Speech

"One last thing on closing, or asking for the job. I know many people who give excellent advice on interviewing. Some have said, 'But asking for the job simply means expressing an interest in the job.'

"Okay, then call it *expressing an interest in the job*. Why say

---

[1] If you are in sales and marketing you may be interested in another book of mine, *The Causes of Sales Success: The Key to Navigating the Maze of Sales*. It applies the ideas in this book, and others, to the complex sales process. For more information, please visit www.tompayne.com.

something that you don't mean? Here is the problem with this imprecise use of language, and I've seen it play out in the real world. People who are relatively new to interviewing will hear someone say, *ask for the job*, and guess what? They actually believe you are meaning what you say. So they walk away thinking they somehow need to ask for the job in their next interview, but they can't figure out how to do this in a way that makes sense.

"From this we can see how the traditional selling model has not only infected interviewing practices, it has created confusion by advocating techniques like closing, or asking for the job, that no one in their right mind uses."

Love It, Like It, or Hate It?

I moved on and asked, "Do you like being interviewed?"

Julie answered, "No. I hate it."

"When you hate something it is difficult to be good at it. So why do you hate interviewing?"

"The pressure, the irrational decisions, the stupid questions… do I need to add to this list?"

"No, that's more than enough. But I'd like to suggest these aren't the real reason you hate interviewing. After all, you like challenges, right?"

This question made Julie smile and say, "I love them."

"But the interview is challenging and you hate it. Why? Because it is the most pressure-packed, complex-sales situation there is; it involves selling the most difficult, complex product: you; and you must face this challenge without ever having received an hour of complex-sales training.

"The closest thing I can liken this to is taking a person who has never driven a car before, showing them where the brake and accelerator pedals are, and then setting them loose on the German autobahn. This is not a challenge; it is a mismatch. It's like sending a 120-pound man into a sumo-wrestling match. No one loves a mismatch because they are unfair. So what we need to do is to make the interview a challenge, instead of a mismatch, and that is where we are headed.

"In our next session we'll look at the mindset that wins even when it loses, and the way to accelerate your growth rate through creative conflict."

Julie used one of her trademark replies: "Bring it."

Lessons

1. Most approaches to interviewing embrace traditional selling techniques, including closing.

2. Traditional selling does not work in a complex sales situation.

3. The interview is a complex-sales situation. It benefits from the use of non-traditional techniques that do not appear sales-y.

4. If we hate interviewing, it is highly likely we will never be very good at it. The real reason why we hate interviews is we are poorly prepared for them. They require skills we've yet to develop and techniques we've yet to master.

3: Setting and Exceeding The Highest Expectations

Rising to the Occasion

I asked Julie, "Are you familiar with the way people typically set low expectations to make it easier for them to exceed them?"

"Indeed I do. I am a master at setting low expectations with a boss and overachieving them. It makes me a hero."

"Congratulations. But with interviewing we need to change this around a bit. We need to set the highest expectations for ourselves and then exceed them."

Julie asked, "Why set yourself up for a demoralizing fall?"

"Two reasons. People tend to perform up to the level of their expectations. When our expectations are high we tend to rise to the occasion. And though we expect to win we may not. In that case we will treat defeat as our honored teacher. Losing is our guide to victory. It will show us how we need to adjust.

"So let's set our expectations right now. What are your expectations for your next interview?"

"That I will win."

"Good! What else?"

"I'm good with *I will win*."

I laughed and said, "Of course you are. But I believe your expectations are too low."

"How do you get higher than winning?"

"How about by winning twice? Multiple offers? Or being so wanted by the hiring authority, or authorities, that you get everything you ask for during the negotiation?"

Julie said, "Okay. That too."

Finding Another Gear

"Excellent. Now we've set the bar high, but how do we clear it? This isn't going to be easy. So how do we take our performance up a notch? How do we find another gear and fly past our competitors?"

"No clue. This sounds like a sports analogy and I'm not big in sports."

"That's okay, because you can still learn from sports. They teach us that ability does not always determine outcome, the best players can lose to the less talented. For example, the Chicago Bulls, our hometown basketball team, show how a mindset can help you elevate your performance to the next level.

"As you may have heard, they lost their MVP player, Derrick Rose, for the 2012-2013 season."

Julie said, "Yes and I'm tired of hearing about it."

"It has been over done, but for the Bulls team it was a devastating loss. Then, during the playoffs, this was followed by the loss of their All-Star small forward, Luol Deng, and starting point guard, Kirk Hinrich. Their All-Star center, Joakim Noah, was hobbled and could only limp up and down the court for several playoff games. They were virtually down three starters and all three of their All-Stars. None of the pundits thought it was possible for them to win, but they did with a group of second and third stringers.

"The secret to the way they exceeded expectations was a big, two-word sign above their locker-room door that says, 'No Excuses.' It became their mindset and it needs to become ours. For the Bulls it meant that when a star got injured the 'next man up' needed to produce, because no one had an excuse for bad results. With his ranks depleted, Coach Tom Thibodeau still repeated his mantra, 'We have more than enough to win.' Everyone else laughed, but his mindset was we have no excuse for losing, and it required his team to find another gear.

"I first encountered this attitude of *no excuses* when I was in the U.S. Army. We were told at least 100 times that the maximum effective range of an excuse was 0.0 meters. Were their mitigating circumstances? Yes. Did they matter? No. This mindset focuses you on producing results, and holding yourself responsible for these results, no matter what."

False Assumption # 3: There Are Legitimate Excuses

"I can see how this mindset can work for an athlete, but not how it translates into the world of interviewing," Julie said.

"It works in the following way. Let's say your resume has weak spots. So what? That's just an excuse. Do something about it. Make it into a strength. For example, I coached a person who was preparing for interviews and she told me interviewers would look at her resume and say, 'you were on such a nice trajectory in the early part of your career. But then, right here,' they would point at a spot on her resume's chronology, 'things changed. What happened?'

"She said this was where the interview always went downhill. She had no good answer for this question that she dreaded. It made her visibly uncomfortable. She wondered, 'What can I do?'

"I thought, 'How about telling them the truth?' So I asked her, 'Okay, what happened?'

"She related to me how her life went through a perfect storm that year. A serious, promising relationship ended, a parent died, and there were a few other personal upsets. She was heartbroken. She said, 'I just needed to take some time off. And so I did some consulting and now I am ready to get back into the corporate fray. But this issue comes up every interview and I don't know what to do about it.'

"I told her to make this weakness a strength and hope they ask about it so she could say:

> Nobody wants to go through really dark and difficult times, but we all experience them to different degrees. The important thing is not how far you get knocked down, but how you respond to the experience. During the time you are asking about I went through a period of personal upheaval that required me to take some time off. So I did. I then worked in a consulting capacity to get back on my feet and learn new skills. This trial did what most trials do. It made me stronger. And now I am ready to reenter the corporate arena and utilize the new skills I've gained.

"Every weakness has a strength. This answer would likely inspire feelings of admiration and the black spot on her resume becomes a memorable story of overcoming adversity.

"She interviewed shortly thereafter and was hired. Remember, no excuses. Ever."

Responsibility and Interviewing

Julie was wrestling with this idea of being responsible for the outcome, no matter what, so she asked, "What if I was just brought in to fill an interviewing quota. What if Human Resources forced the hiring authority to interview at least three people, but the hiring authority knew beforehand she was going to hire her friend? Is my interviewing failure my fault even when the decision is foreordained."

"Of course it is. Un-foreordain this decision. Show this person and *everyone else you interview with* why you are a far better choice.

"Take this example. You don't get any more foreordained than this. The First International Tchaikovsky Competition in 1958 occurred in Moscow at the height of the Cold War. Its purpose was to prove the cultural superiority of the communist state. The winning pianist was foreordained. The fix was in. Then a young Texan performed and received a standing ovation that lasted eight minutes.

"The officials did not know what to do. They knew Van Cliburn had won, and they knew they lived in a state with a very large Gulag. So they asked the Soviet leader, Nikita Khrushchev, if it was okay to award him this prize. Khrushchev asked if he had won. They said he did. Khrushchev probably shocked them with his response, 'Give him the prize.' What was thought to be foreordained was not.

"Now if he had lost, a no-excuses attitude would have asked, 'What can I do to improve?'

"Everyone can improve their performance. The failure to produce results is an indicator that improvement is needed. But there is a big obstacle standing in the way of our improvement. Sometimes it is difficult to figure out what we did wrong, or are doing wrong, because we can't step outside of our body and see our self during the interview. So how do we overcome this obstacle?"

Julie said, "Have someone help you find out what's wrong. Like what we're doing here."

"You got it, Julie. Jobseekers need a coach. A trained set of eyes watching them and recommending corrective actions."

Taking Charge

"But what does coaching have to do with responsibility?" Julie asked. "Isn't getting a coach a shifting of responsibility to someone else?"

"It's the exact opposite. Multi-million dollar athletes have coaches help them with their golf swing, or the way they swing a bat. Is anyone going to hold them less responsible when they keep missing fairways or striking out?

"It's your responsibility to improve, and no one else's. Few things accelerate this process better than working with a coach. Why might that be?"

"I guess it's their objectivity. I know I am biased about myself, so I might not see my issues as clearly as a coach."

"Yes, that is critical, but so is this. A coach provides a different perspective and this simple element is at the core of high-performance teams. These teams are greater than the sum of their parts. In other words, on my own I may have a performance grade of 6.5. But when I am part of this team my performance level jumps to 10. Then, when I leave my team, my performance level drops to 6.5 again, because I no longer have the advantage of the team's different perspectives.

"We all need the unique perspectives of others because we all have blind spots. The interview coach sees what the jobseeker cannot.

"When I do consulting work on the subject of team building I tell the client that the goal of a team is to develop a bond of trust and respect to unleash the power of creative conflict. I'll give you an example of what I mean."

The Power of Creative Conflict

"The songwriting team of John Lennon and Paul McCartney is one of the best illustrations of the power of creative conflict that I've ever come across. Their productivity, and the quality of their work, is perhaps unrivalled in modern music history. Some of their hits are."

I then read from a list:

> I Want To Hold Your Hand
> A Hard Day's Night
> Ticket To Ride
> Help!
> Yesterday
> Penny Lane
> All You Need Is Love
> Lady Madonna
> Hey Jude
> Something
> Come Together
> Let It Be

No Medal For Second Place

The Long And Winding Road
A Day In The Life

Julie said, "They were before my time, but their music is still good. That's an amazing list."

"And it's a partial list. Now here is an example of how this team utilized creative conflict to achieve better results. McCartney wrote a song that began:

Well, she was just seventeen,
Never been a beauty queen…

"And Lennon said, 'You're joking about that line aren't you?'

"To Lennon this line needed a little edge, but McCartney couldn't see this on his own. He was the incarnation of sunny, pop-oriented music while Lennon, on the other hand, had an edgier, bluesy sensibility. Their perspectives were completely different and this is one reason why they were such a powerful team. They balanced each other. So Lennon, in line with his unique perspective, offered the following improvement:

Well, she was just seventeen,
You know what I mean.

"A note of sexual suggestion entered the song and a forgettable line became memorable.

"Individuals in a team with creative conflict are more powerful together than they are apart. This was certainly true of McCartney and Lennon. When they stopped working together their music suffered in terms of both quantity and quality. Much of McCartney's music became sappy pop without Lennon's influence. 'Silly Love Songs,' 'Band on the Run,' can't compare to the songs he wrote when teamed with Lennon. Once they parted both suffered a drop in productivity and quality.

"It's sad, but the differences people have tend to tear teams apart when they should be the source of the team's greatest strength. But unless the team is bound together by trust and respect these differences become destructive.

"When Lennon said, 'You're joking about that line aren't you?'

McCartney knew it was not said to insult him, or hurt his feelings, but to make his song better. That was the reason why they were meeting. He trusted Lennon. He also knew he needed to listen; Lennon's rare musical ability was worthy of respect.

"They were young, but remarkably mature individuals. They didn't just allow for candid, constructive criticism, they sought it."

Destructive Conflict

"But when the bond of trust doesn't exist the conflict is not creative, it's destructive. A perfect example of this was captured in the 'Let It Be' documentary film. In this film McCartney tried to engage George Harrison in the same sort of creative conflict that he and Lennon enjoyed, but Harrison wanted nothing to do with it. He became visibly stressed and engaged in submissive behavior, by saying to McCartney, 'I'll play whatever you want me to play, or I won't play at all if you don't want me to play. Whatever it is that'll please you, I'll do it.'

"He left the band a few days later. He eventually returned, but the break-up of the Beatles was playing out before the cameras."

I paused for a moment and looked at Julie until she got a little fidgety and asked, "What?"

I answered, "Fasten your seat belt. This next false assumption is one of the deadliest, because it seems so normal and non-threatening."

False Assumption # 4: My Attitude Is Fine

"There are winning and losing attitudes. In the job-search world one of the losing attitudes can be expressed as follows: 'I am unemployed and seeking a job.' Now that sounds harmless and normal enough, doesn't it?"

Julie answered, "Yes," without adding her usual color commentary. I could tell she was intrigued and wanted to know how this could possibly be one of the most dangerous assumptions.

" 'I am unemployed and seeking a job' sounds normal and harmless because it appears to be merely conveying the facts of a person's situation. But what it is saying between the lines is this: I am defined by what I lack, namely, a job, and when I think of how best to describe myself I think, 'I am unemployed.'

"When a jobseeker start to think of himself in negative terms he becomes less assertive. He goes from being a productive contributor to being a needy person waiting for work to materialize.

" 'I am a problem seeking a solution' is another way of saying, 'I am unemployed and seeking a job.' As this attitude takes root it begins to stand in the way of positive, productive action. Let me illustrate how this works.

"One of the people I was coaching said, 'I'm going to a meeting next week and this important person in our city government will be there. He has tons of connections, but I bet he gets asked about job opportunities all of the time. So, I probably shouldn't waste my time asking him about opportunities, should I?'

"His words said, 'I am just another problem. Who would want to see me?' The answer is, 'No one,' unless you change your I-am-not-worth-seeing attitude. His defeatism was proving the maxim: *The war we must win is fought within.*

"This is not only a war we must win, it's a war we can win. We just need to adopt an attitude that is the exact opposite of, 'I am a problem seeking a solution.' We change it into, 'I am a solution seeking problems.'

"Notice how this shifts our thinking away from what we lack toward what we can offer. We go from being retiring, pathetic creatures who receive pity instead of job offers, into positive people who hold their heads high and shout, 'What are your problems, hiring authority? Because I want to explore how I can help you solve them.'

"And here's the thing. This positive attitude is every bit as reality-based as its negative cousin. After all, we *really* do have valuable abilities and skills. By focusing on the value we bring we exude success pheromones and become an overwhelmingly attractive candidate to a hiring authority.

"Does this make sense?"

"Yes, it makes sense," Julie replied as she pursed her lips. "It makes too much sense. And it hurts to hear this since I've been playing a down-in-the-mouth victim for the last few months. What you're telling me should have been so obvious to me, but I didn't see it."

"Julie, don't be hard on yourself. When you get kicked in the teeth, it's the most natural thing in the world to think about your missing teeth. Besides, your ability to reason this out was no match for the emotions of fear, anger or depression. We can't see clearly when we are emotionally upset. That's one of the reasons why jobseekers need friends, a support group, and a coach."

The Advantage of Coaching

"Look," Julie said, "I can see the value of having a coach and being coached. But can't you just teach yourself how to interview, network and all that other job search stuff?"

"Yes, and some are better at teaching themselves than others. But coaches accelerate growth. An individual might take six months to a year to take his interviewing skills to a high level. But if this same person had a coach it might take him 1-2 weeks to reach an even higher level.

"Also, we need to have our existing ideas challenged. We all have a certain way of looking at things and this limits us to producing more of the same. For example, when a jobseeker rehearses by himself he may refine his performance, but he is unlikely to make dramatic changes, and dramatic change may be necessary."

"How about using a friend as a coach?" Julie asked.

"The problem with a friend is the way he will filter his feedback to protect your feelings. Sometimes candid, unfiltered criticism is the only thing that will get a person to change their course. When I go over how I helped a bitter person overcome expressing his bitterness you will see how even the most obvious, candid criticism fails to get through to some people. A filtered critique makes this communication problem worse.

"Also, don't our best friends tend to see things the same way we do? Isn't that one of the reasons why we hang around them? This similarity of perspectives minimizes the power of creative conflict. Different perspectives are what we need to help us see what we can't see on our own. My perspective is different from yours because of my expertise."

"But coaching is expensive."

Julie brought up an important point. Executive outplacement offers coaching, but these packages can start at $5,000 and go up from there. However, excellent, low-cost options exist. So I pulled out a sheet of paper detailing a few of these options and handed it to her. It appears in the Appendix.

Julie looked over the sheet and said, "I had no idea there were affordable services like this."

"Yes. They offer real value. Now in our next session we will finish laying the foundation and then begin to build on it. Are you ready?"

"As ready as I'll ever be."

Lessons

1. You are responsible for every interviewing outcome.

2. There may be mitigating circumstances, but refuse to accept any excuses.

3. You are not a burden, a problem seeking a solution. You are a valuable solution to a hiring authority's problems, and you need to act like it.

4. Jobseekers benefit from a coach. We cannot see ourselves perform and different perspectives can see important things that we cannot.

5. Worse yet, without a coach our minds can play tricks on us as the next chapter shows.

4: Perception Is…
More Important than Reality

Julie seemed to be settling down. She looked more relaxed and comfortable. Unfortunately, I had to rock her conceptual world once again. I said, "You'll probably reject what I'm going to share with you next."

"You won't know until you tell me. So go ahead. Hit me with your best shot."

False Assumption # 5: Substance Is More Important than Style

We both smiled and then I said, "Here it is: Style is far more important than substance in an interview. Or, to put it another way, how we appear, and the way we say things, has far more influence on an interviewer than who we actually are or what we've achieved."

Julie erupted, "No way!"

I shot back, "Yes way! But I confess, I rejected this too. After all, who wants to embrace a statement that essentially says, 'I'm superficial and shallow and so is everyone else'?

"I'm still not buying it. What changed your mind?"

"My experience and the experiences of others. The following is a case study that illustrates the way style trumps substance."

Case Study

"It comes from research conducted by authors Neil Rackham and Richard Ruff. They were observing salespeople, but the results of their study apply to interviewing as well.

"They interviewed salespeople to determine what their real thoughts and feelings were. They also interviewed their customers to find out their feelings about these salespeople. The following is how a salesperson named David felt."

I then read David's response during an interview:

> I joined this corporation because it pays me best. …I don't believe in its products—they are overpriced and have no better features than the competition. I'm not interested in customers. As far as I'm concerned, I'm in this job for two years. I'm going to make a killing and move on. When I look at a customer I don't see a face, I just see my commission paycheck. I'm prepared to do or say anything which will get some fool to sign money into my pocket.[2]

Julie said, "People like David give me the creeps. It's why I could never make it in sales."

I replied, "You may not have what it takes to be a good salesperson, but don't mistake David for some archetype of salespeople. I've worked in sales all my life and find the vast majority of salespeople to be honest, hardworking and fun to be around.

"Now let's compare David to Alan."

I then read Alan's response during an interview:

> I really believe in this company and its products… and I think we try to achieve the best for our customers. In the

---

[2] Neil Rackham, Richard Ruff, *Managing Major Sales: Practical Strategies for Improving Sales Effectiveness* (New York: Harper Business, 1991), pp. 96-97.

eight years I've been in this job, the client has always come first, and I believe that sales success depends on a real and genuine desire to help each customer.[3]

I looked up from the case study and asked, "Who was the more sincere of the two?"

Julie shot back, "Why even ask when the answer is so obvious?"

"Please, humor me."

"Okay. Alan is more sincere." And then she quickly added, "Now don't tell me I'm wrong on this one too."

"You are wrong."

"C'mon! Stop doing this to me! I can't be wrong, can I?"

"In the world of reality, Alan is more sincere than David. So in this world you answered correctly. But in the world of interviews and sales, the real world is less important than the unreal world of perception. This is because everyone lives in this reality-bending world of perception. In this world, David was perceived to be more sincere than Alan, and here is the reason why."

I then finished reading the case study:

> David was a master of the firm handshake, steady eye contact, a relaxed open posture, the concerned smile and reassuring words. All of these things were behaviors—the customer could see them and be influenced by them. Alan, on the other hand, tended to avoid eye contact. He would sit hunched up, he would be jerky in his speech, and he would say things like, "I can't really answer you." In short his behaviors gave the impression he was concealing something—so customers judged him insincere. The conclusions are simple. Customers judge by what they can see.[4]

"In the real world Alan was sincere, but this did not matter when it came time for customers to make buying decisions. Sincere Alan

---

[3] Neil Rackham, Richard Ruff, p. 97.
[4] Neil Rackham, Richard Ruff, p. 97.

sold a whopping 30% less than insincere David, because David's behaviors generated the perception that he was trustworthy while Alan's did the opposite.

"Perception is more important than reality for the salesperson and for the jobseeker. When it comes to the hiring decision, who you really are is unimportant when compared to how you are perceived. Julie, you were *really* better than Jane, who was hired, but reality doesn't cause the hiring decision. Since this unreal world of perception is the one that matters in a job interview, your answer was wrong. From an interviewing perspective, David was more sincere.

Lessons From the Case Study

"This case study shows us how appearance trumps essence and style overpowers substance, and it brings to mind the popular saying: *Perception is reality*.

"But as we've seen, perception is not reality. The perception is David is sincere and Alan is not. The reality is the exact opposite. When people say, 'Perception is reality,' I think they actually mean, 'Perception is an individual's reality,' and this makes it more powerful than what is actually real.

"There is a chain of causation that unfolds as follows. My behaviors lead to perceptions that lead to emotions that cause hiring decisions. But always remember, the chain begins with behavior, what the hiring authority sees and hears, the outside not the inside."

The Objection

Julie was squirming in her chair. She couldn't take it any longer and finally exclaimed, "If your approach is all about appearing to be someone you're not, then count me out. If I have to finish second place for the rest of my life, I'm okay with that."

"Julie," I said, "I would never ask you to be deceptive. David is simply an illustration of the way our behaviors shape perceptions and perceptions generate emotions like trust."

"Yes, but why can't what is real and valuable, win out over fluff or style? This is disturbing."

"Yes, it is. It is another example of why the wrong assumptions rule in the world of interviewing. We prefer the lie because it is easier to accept than the truth. But we can't change human nature, or how we perceive things, we simply have to deal with it.

"This area is one where most interviewing guides provide valuable information. Think about the things that David did, but Alan did not. He maintained eye contact, had a relaxed, open posture, and gave a firm handshake. These are the same things almost every interviewing guide tells their readers to do. In this case they are all running in the right direction. But I don't think they take this principle of *style trumping substance* far enough.

"Every answer to every question during the interview is a behavior that can be made more powerful by attending to its style. And we'll cover that in just a little while."

Julie replied, "Then, based on what you are telling me, the substance of your answer is less important than the style of your answer. Is that right?"

"Much less important. Now to finish laying the foundation there is one more mental mechanism we need to understand."

First Impressions And Mindsets

"We all know that first impressions are important, but why? Why do they set the tone for the many personal interactions that follow? Why are bad first impressions hard to overcome?"

Julie thought about this for a moment and said, "I'm not sure. I suppose they shape what a person expects to see. If I act in a certain way, then they probably expect more of the same. Right?"

"Very good! I am impressed. These expectations are the result of something that is called a mindset. Mindsets have the following characteristics: They are quick to form, resist change, and assimilate all additional information to conform to the existing image.[5]

"Here is how the mindset, called a first impression, works. If my mindset is *you are an honest person*, then I will overlook it when you tell me something I know to be untrue. I will think, 'She just made an honest mistake.' In other words, your falsehood was reinterpreted to fit the pre-existing image I had of you. I expect you to be honest and I bend reality to fit this expectation. Mindsets, therefore, have a powerful influence on perception.

"Now take a look at the following image and tell me what you see."

I handed her a sheet with this image:

"What do you see?"

"I see 'Paris in the spring.' "

"Most people see the same thing. Only it doesn't say that. It says, 'Paris in the *the* spring,' 'Once in a *a* lifetime,' and 'Bird in the *the* hand.' "

---

[5] Richards J. Heuer, Jr., *Psychology of Intelligence Analysis,* (Center for the Study of Intelligence, CIA, 1999), pp. 10, 11. This book is now out of print and this quote comes from a pdf that is available at www.odci.gov/csi.

"Wow! That's weird."

"It is. And it reflects the way we are wired. We see the familiar phrase that we expect to see, not the phrase that is actually there. The interviewer's perceptions generate mindsets, and he begins to see what he expects to see. Mindsets are more important than reality in an interview, because they bend reality to fit their image.

"I got this picture from a book written for CIA intelligence analysts. It said the following about the 'Paris in the spring' picture:

> Did you perceive Figure 1 correctly? If so, you have exceptional powers of observation, were lucky, or have seen the figure before. This simple experiment demonstrates one of the most fundamental principles concerning perception:
>
> **We tend to perceive what we expect to perceive.**[6]

"Mindsets expect to see certain things and shape our perceptions, perceptions then generate emotions, and emotions cause hiring decisions. So if our goal is to cause a hiring decision, then we must establish favorable mindsets through expressing specific behaviors.

"Another important twist to how we perceive things is this: 'perception is affected not only by what people *expect* to see; it is also colored by what they *want* to see.'[7]

"So how do we get the hiring authority to *want to see* us succeed in our interview? We achieve this end by forging a positive emotional connection with him. This entire interviewing system is geared to achieve this end."

Objections Resurface

"This is starting to make me feel uneasy," Julie said. "It's like you are opening the door to mental tricks that can be used to fool someone."

---

[6] Heuer, p. 8.
[7] Scott Plous, *The Psychology of Judgment and Decision Making* (New York: McGraw Hill, 1993), p. 18.

"You can look at it that way. Or you can look at it like this. Until we understand how our minds work, how perceptions are formed, we might be unwittingly sabotaging ourselves. Take Alan and David. Do you think Alan wanted to be perceived as being deceptive?"

"No. Alan seemed to be a sweet man."

"Agreed. But if he knew how his behaviors created negative perceptions, and changed these behaviors, then his customers would have seen him as he really is. Would this be fooling people or somehow tricking them?

"No."

"Right you are, Julie. Now let's put you in this picture. You were more talented and successful than Jane, but the interviewer's perception was that you were a second-place candidate. Like Alan, your behaviors betrayed you, and your inside was not matched by your outside; your style failed to express your competence and achievement and we need to change that."

The Power of Mindsets

"One last thing about mindsets. They stand guard over the status quo, because they resist change. A reason why people cling to their wrong assumptions, even in the face of evidence that refutes them, is because their mindsets re-interpret this evidence to fit the existing image. Have you experienced that?"

Julie almost shouted, "Yes! When you asked what causes the hiring decision I kept thinking it was having better achievements than my competitor. Then I would remember my recent interviewing experience and think, 'This can't be right, because my achievements did not result in me being hired.' But my mind kept returning to this same thought, 'Achievements cause the hiring decision,' even after I'd discredited it.

"I said to myself, 'I can't think outside the box because I am the box.' "

"Our mindsets are the boxes and they are difficult for us to change on our own. This is why a coach and creative conflict are often needed. McCartney lived in his own box as did Lennon, but neither lived in the other person's box. They were able to provide real, out-of-the-box thinking for each other and it produced musical magic.

"Mindsets are powerful and they can work against you unless you know about them and use them to your advantage."

"When do I start learning how to do this?"

"Tomorrow. The foundation is now in place. Tomorrow we start building on it. Are you ready?"

Julie said, "I'm ready." And she was.

Lessons

1. Style trumps substance in an interview. How we appear, and the way we answer questions, is more powerful than who we are or what we've achieved.

2. Our concern is with behaviors, because they shape perceptions, perceptions generate emotions and emotions cause hiring decisions.

3. First impressions are critical during an interview since they are mindsets that form quickly, resist change and assimilate new information to fit the preexisting image.

4. To improve our performance we need to change, but our mindsets resist change. We need creative conflict, or new ideas from an outside source. Books can provide these, but few things are as effective as knowledgeable coaches.

Section Two:

The Interview

5: First Impressions

Julie was running about fifteen minutes late for our meeting. I heard a hurried knock, opened the door and saw she was agitated. She entered the door, quickly collected herself and said, "I'm sorry I'm late. I got a last second call from a recruiter and it looks like I will be interviewing next week."

Before I could respond she said, "I hate being late."

"Me too, but don't worry about it. You were taking care of important business and I couldn't be happier for you."

"You mentioned how this preparation process requires a lot of work. Do we have enough time to get ready?"

"We could use a little more time. But we have more than enough to give you some powerful advantages. Shall we get started?"

"Let's get at it."

"Alright, the last time we met we spoke about that quirky little mental process called a mindset. Do you remember?"

"Yes. They form quickly, resist change and assimilate all new information to fit the existing image."

"Wow! Good job. Now the mindset you create in the interviewer's mind typically begins with the first meeting. But sometimes it is set in place based on phone screenings, emails or a dynamite resume, letters of recommendation and the like.

"I was working on an international consulting assignment and the prep work required several emails between me and the members of my seminar. I remember clearly how these emails expressed their personalities and formed a first impression. So be on your best behavior whether you are speaking on the phone, emailing someone, or meeting for the first time. The goal of these behaviors is to create an impression that you are a likable, confident and competent person.

"You don't have any problems with trying to be likable, do you Julie?"

"Moi? Of course not. Everyone loves me."

"I have no doubt. But I think we can make you even more likable by adding a behavior to your repertoire that I have not seen very often. A smile."

Behavioral Elements Of First Impressions

Smile

Julie forced a smile and said, "That hurts my face."

I laughed and was glad she was able to clown around a little. It showed she wasn't too uptight as she headed into her interview prep-work. "You'll get used to smiling," I said, "and you must, because smiles have an emotional impact on the person who is smiling and the person who sees this smile.

"When someone yawns everyone around him yawns, and when someone smiles people tend to smile in return. This is important, because the physical act of smiling actually generates positive emotions in the person who smiles."

She said, "Wait a minute. Do you mean to tell me you actually believe that my smile will cause someone else to smile, and then this physical movement of her lips will cause her to feel positive emotions as a result?"

"I couldn't have said it any better."

"Then prove it."

I pulled out a paper detailing research into the impact people's facial expressions had on their emotional state and read:

> A spate of recent studies of botox recipients and others suggests that our emotions are reinforced—perhaps even driven—by their corresponding facial expressions.

> ...This February [in 2009] psychologists at the University of Cardiff in Wales found that people whose ability to frown is compromised by cosmetic botox injections are happier, on average, than people who can frown. The researchers administered an anxiety and depression questionnaire to 25 females, half of whom had received frown-inhibiting botox injections. The botox recipients reported feeling happier and less anxious in general; more important, they did not report feeling any more attractive, which suggests that the emotional effects were not driven by a psychological boost that could come from the treatment's cosmetic nature.

> "It would appear that the way we feel emotions isn't just restricted to our brain—there are parts of our bodies that help and reinforce the feelings we're having," says Michael Lewis, a co-author of the study. "It's like a feedback loop." In a related study from March, scientists at the Technical University of Munich in Germany scanned botox recipients with fMRI machines while asking them to mimic angry faces. They found that the botox subjects had much lower activity in the brain circuits involved in emotional processing and responses—in the amygdala, hypothalamus and parts of the brain stem—as compared with controls who had not received treatment.[8]

Julie looked at me and said, "You've got to be kidding me."

"No, I'm not. Princeton University developed a facial expression

---

[8] Melinda Wenner, Smile: *It Could Make You Happier* (originally appearing in the Scientific American magazine, October 14, 2009). Quoted from the online article. The online link: www.scientificamerican. com/article.cfm?id=smile-it-could-make-you-happier.

chart that ranged from the most-trustworthy face to the least, and the most obvious difference between the two pictures was a smile on the most-trustworthy face and a frown on the least-trustworthy face. In other words, the critical emotion of trust was, in part, generated by a smile while the emotion of distrust was similarly caused by a frown.

"I imagine you go into your interview and you are all business, looking seriouser than a heart attack."

"Now that's serious," Julie observed and continued, "I probably do look serious and intense, because I don't like interviewing. So yeah, I don't smile a lot during an interview."

"It's a simple behavior and its absence is hurting your interviewing chances.

"Now, at the risk of bringing up an unpleasant subject, could you describe Jane for me? Is she an intense person?"

"The exact opposite. Always smiling…"

I interrupted, "And though you are the more substantial candidate, Jane finished first. I'm sure she did more than smile, but her pleasant behaviors created the perception that she was… pleasant."

Julie said without a trace of humor in her voice, "I hate Jane."

"That brings up another important point. I want to share a story about a bitter person I helped get hired. I referred to him earlier when I spoke about how some people are unable to hear candid, accurate criticism."

Calling Bitter, Party of One!

"Jack had no problem getting an interview. Everyone who looked at his resume of achievements wanted him on their team…until they met him. During interviews they would discover he had a tape replaying in his head about how he was treated so unfairly by his last boss. It was so unjust! He had a right to be angry! The interview would end and the tape in his head rewound until it returned to its root of bitterness. He loved his bitterness, snuggled up next to it, and refused to let it go.

"Do you know why 'Bitter' is always a party of one?"

Julie answered, "It's because no one wants to be around a bitter person."

"You got that right. I got a chance to meet Jack at an employment workshop I was conducting pro-bono at my church. I was going over how you need to be universally positive during your interview, because positive emotions tend to generate positive emotions, while negative ones generate the bad vibes that result in someone else winning the job.

"I then said:

> I don't care if you're last boss was unjust, unfair, a nasty tyrant who should never manage another soul. If you've had a boss like this, and the interviewer asks you, "How would you describe your last boss?" You respond, "He was a great teacher. I learned more from him than possibly any other boss I've worked for." And you say this because he did teach you not to do the things he did. Remember to never be negative.

"Jack exploded, 'I couldn't say that. I couldn't say anything positive about a man who lied compulsively and treated me the way he did.'

"I asked Jack, 'Have you ever expressed this bitterness during an interview?'

"He thought about it and said, 'Yes, I suppose I have.'

"I asked, 'Since your bad experience with your former boss, have you ever made it to the second round of interviews?'

"He answered, 'No.'

"I then explained how bitterness was an interview killer, and how no interviewer cared about his bitterness and anger, except in this way: It's not their problem and they want to keep it that way. 'So they don't hire you,' I said, and then asked, 'Now would you choose someone who was bitter and angry over someone who was charming and positive?'

"Jack wasn't about to let go of his bitterness without a fight. He said, 'I would choose the person with the best skills.'

"Like many people, he thought his credentials and achievements would cause the hiring decision. So I said, 'But you know the most qualified person does not always get the job offer. I bet you were more accomplished than every candidate who was hired instead of you.

" 'So why do interviewers bypass better-qualified candidates? It is because the hiring decision is emotional, not rational, and bitterness is emotionally repulsive. Until you get over your bitterness, no one will hire you.'

"He still resisted accepting responsibility for his interviewing failures. His false assumptions, mindsets and arrogance kept him from seeing what seemed so obvious to me, so I said to the workshop attendees, 'We are not here to gang up on Jack; we are here to help him. It could be I am misreading him entirely. Does anyone else feel he is expressing his bitterness in a way that might prevent his being hired?'

"They supported my view, and our consensus opened Jack's eyes. I concluded with this advice, 'Try to do only one thing in your next interview. Emanate warmth and see what happens.'

"Days later he was interviewed for the umpteenth time and was hired."

Julie interjected, "Jack does not sound like he was a pleasant person."

"I can assure you he wasn't. And I can clearly remember two of his behaviors. He was extremely intense and he never smiled."

Julie winced as I described him. She began to see how her behaviors made her appear to be too more like Jack and less like Julie.

So I added, "Julie, you are a nice, likable person, but your interviewing behaviors fail to express this. I want to change that. I want the outer Julie to match the inner Julie."

"Good luck with that," she smirked.

"You are right. I will need a little luck. It's not because you are such a tough case. Jack was a lot tougher and he was hired the next time he interviewed. But behavior change is very difficult. Think about dieting, or exercising. It's tough to develop positive, new behavioral habits; but as Jack proved, it can be done.

"But before we go on, I need you to commit to being only positive and never negative during an interview. Okay?"

"I'm on board."

"Good. Always be positive. It will make a difference."

Confidence

"Some people who are interviewing have been beaten up by previous interviewing experiences. Others are beaten down by life. They are emotionally raw and possess no confidence. They express weariness without saying a word. Does this sound at all like you?"

Julie answered, "I want my mojo back."

"We'll get it back. Most people would think I had few reasons to be confident when I interviewed for that great opportunity on the West Coast. But I confidently looked forward to the interview and I enjoyed it. This was the result of many long hours of preparation.

"To be confident, be prepared. It's worth the effort, because radiating confidence is more powerful than a dozen great achievements on a resume. This is because of the way we are like emotional tuning forks. Someone else's emotional tone gets us to vibrate the same way. Our confidence makes the interviewer confident in us."

Style Matters: What You Wear

"William Shakespeare once wrote, 'The apparel oft proclaims the man,'[9] and this is certainly true for men and women during an interview. Clothes pack a powerful emotional punch, so if you have an undiagnosed, fashion disability seek professional help."

"What on earth are you talking about?" Julie asked.

"Simple. Most people wear clothing to an interview that is less

---

[9] William Shakespeare, *Hamlet*, Act I, Scene iii, l. 72.

than optimal. Their style choices range from OMG to OK. So unless you are always complimented on your style of dress, go to a store specializing in fine business attire, or casual office wear, and ask the staff for assistance. It is their business to know what is working and what is not, and how to accessorize an outfit. A tired, dated appearance can hurt you.

Then I added, "Julie, your clothes look fine to me, but I'm no fashion expert and you interview in a few days. So I would go out today and get expert advice. Wear the outfit you plan on wearing to the interview and go to either…" I then mentioned several high-end stores that carried women's business attire. "Then ask a salesperson if they think your outfit is a good choice for an interview. Most people will give good and honest advice. They know what an interview is like and want to help.

"If they say you need an update because your outfit is no longer in style, then indulge yourself. Clothing is important. Don't underestimate its impact."

Julie confessed, "I've never been one to pay too much attention to fashion, but I know I need to. Expert advice couldn't hurt."

I continued, "Fashion norms are part of a company's culture and we should never insult them. At some companies a suit will make you look like an alien from outer space. But never assume business attire is inappropriate, even at a casual company. I once wore a suit to an interview, and was expected to, while the interviewer wore jeans.

"If you have doubts about the dress code, then call the company's Human Resources department and ask."

"Just call right out of the blue and ask? That sounds like it is a good way to disqualify yourself before you even get there."

Julie's questioning revealed how her perspective was different from mine. She didn't realize, until later, how we were constantly engaged in creative conflict. I was helping her to think outside of her box.

"Disqualify yourself?" I questioned, "The exact opposite is the case. You are basically saying I want to respect your cultural norms."

"So what do you say? How do you pull that off? It just sounds so awkward."

"Simple. I'd say, 'Hi, my name is Tom and I'm going to be visiting your headquarters for an interview tomorrow. Since dress codes are so different from place to place I'd just like to ask if business attire would be appropriate, or does your company prefer a candidate dress casually for their interview?'

"Most people will help you. They don't want you to stumble right out of the gate for something silly.

"No matter what their dress code, wear your best quality clothing. This applies to business or casual attire.

Upon Arrival

"I'll close this session with a few fairly obvious points that you've likely heard before, but they are worth remembering.

"One way to make a bad first impression is to be late for your interview. If it is due to circumstances outside of your control (for example, a four-hour delay at the airport), then don't worry about it. In those situations give the hiring authority updates on your progress and stay calm. When you arrive with a big smile you will impress the hiring authority with the way you can keep your cool during a stressful time. Your bad situation will help you make a better first impression than you would have if you'd been on time. This is the power of always being positive and turning weaknesses into strengths.

"But when possible, arrive at least five to ten minutes early. Find a bathroom, and check to make sure your hair is in place and your clothing is in order.

"Finally, at some companies the receptionist is part of the interview. They want to know if you treat this person with the same respect that you show the hiring authority.

"A powerful approach is to walk up to the receptionist and imagine he or she is your first interview. Practice your smile and warm introduction, and then have a seat and confidently wait for someone to escort you to your first interview."

Lessons

1. Smile.

2. Always be positive, even about negative things.

3. Confidence is the child of preparation.

4. The clothing you wear is a powerful shaper of perceptions. Be up-to-date in your attire.

5. Everyone in the hiring company can be part of the interview.

6. Tell Me a Story

It's amazing how people resist using one of the most powerful interviewing tools: Presenting your accomplishments in a story format. Julie was no different. After I said, "Julie, now we will study how to present your achievements through the medium of stories," she asked, "Why?"

Julie was an analytical sort. Sharing facts and data was her preferred communication style. She thought stories were inefficient, and filled with irrelevant details. She wondered, "What purpose could they serve?" She was about to find out.

I continued, "Do you remember when I told you about how I out-interviewed someone who was far more qualified than me?"

"Yes, and I've been waiting for you to tell me how you did it. Are you finally going to let the cat out of the bag?"

"Sure. Why not? The funny thing is their hiring decision also shocked me. So, about a month after being hired, I approached my boss and asked her, 'Why did you hire me instead of the other guy?'

"She said, 'You had such great stories.' In other words, the stories I used to convey my accomplishments caused her to hire me and—do not miss this—*she remembered their impact a month later.* Meanwhile, my competition's sterling qualifications were not as powerful as my stories for reasons that will become plain."

I always knew where I stood with Julie. She said, "Don't stories take too long to get to the point? I think it's great the way they worked for you, but I don't really like stories."

"I bet you do," I replied, "Do you like the TV show *60 Minutes* with all of its wonderful facts and data about newsworthy events?"

"Of course."

"It is one of the highest-rated TV shows in American TV history," I continued, "and it became a huge success by turning news into stories. This was no accident. The show's creator, Don Hewitt, lived by a simple motto that he said was contained in these four little words, 'Tell me a story.' So you see, even though you are an analytical type, you still enjoy a good story. And there are reasons why you do and why they work during interviews.

"Let me give you an example of how a story can be used during an interview."

"By all means," Julie replied.

Data-Point Vs. Story

"In manufacturing there is a measurement of quality. If your quality level is one error per 1,000 opportunities, then it is appalling. If it is improved five hundredfold to one error per 500,000 opportunities, then your quality has just taken a big step in the right direction. It is an achievement worth highlighting in a story.

"During an interview our manufacturing person, Bob, was asked, 'What achievement are you proudest of?'

"Bob could answer this question with a stark, cold fact: 'I'm proudest of the way I improved the quality of our production process. I reduced the error rate from one error per 1,000 opportunities to one per 500,000.' This captures the substance of his impressive achievement in a forgettable style. It's a fact that will get lost in the deluge of facts that he and the other candidates will dump on the suffering interviewer. But when this achievement becomes a story a forgettable fact becomes memorable:

What am I proudest of? When I joined Acme the company had a reputation for putting out the lowest-quality product in our industry, and the manufacturing team had high turnover and very low morale.

To turn this situation around I developed a plan with measurable milestones and whenever we achieved one we would have a mini-celebration. We focused on process improvements and began to build quality into the product.

Before you knew it, we became a team and the quality gains we produced were dramatic. We reduced the failure rate five hundredfold. Instead of one error per 1,000 opportunities it became one per 500,000. This reduced the cost of manufactured goods by 10%. Margins improved for the first time in five years. The estimated annual impact was $200,000 to the bottom line. And our internal surveys showed my manufacturing team went from being among the least satisfied employees to the most satisfied in the company.

"Now imagine you are the one who is conducting the interview. Which answer—the dry data-point or the story—would prove to be the most interesting and memorable?

"You may interview against more accomplished people, but if your achievements are fleshed out in a story, and theirs aren't, then yours will appear larger than theirs. For example, a competitor for this manufacturing position might say, 'I am proudest of the fact that I reduced the error rate from one every 1,000 opportunities, to one every 1,000,000.' This is twice as good as Bob's achievement yet it seems less powerful than his story about the way he turned his demoralized team around and produced big gains to the bottom line."

Why Tell a Story?

I pulled out another sheet of paper that summarized why a story was such a powerful interviewing tool and handed it to Julie. It read as follows:

1. Stories can make your smaller achievements seem larger

than the more substantial achievements of your competitors.

2. Stories are entertaining. People, who are entertaining, are more likable than those who bore interviewers with endless statistics, facts and data.

3. Stories are memorable. Most people can remember stories from their childhood.

4. Good stories hook the interviewer's attention and hold it. If you are the fourth interview of the day, this can be critical.

5. Some people are more visual than others. Stories enable you to communicate more effectively to them.

6. Stories enable you to stand apart from your competitors who probably aren't using this technique.

7. Stories make self-promotion palatable. You don't sound like you are boasting or selling.

8. Stories are digestible. A story's context helps the mind assess the magnitude and importance of the achievement.

"So Julie, will you give stories a chance?"

"Yes. What made a difference for me was the way your story didn't seem touchy-feely. But I was surprised by the amount of facts and data you used. Isn't that running in the wrong direction?"

"Sometimes it is, but not in this story. The interviewer might forget most of the data I added to the end of this story, but the overall impact would be, 'Wow! The numbers he produced. Impressive!' "

Data Dump Vs. Story

"We've seen how the story makes a much stronger impact than the data-point. Let's now look at how it compares to the following data-dump:

> I'm proudest of the way I improved the quality of our manufacturing process from one defect per 1,000 opportunities to one defect per 500,000 opportunities. The steps taken to achieve this were many. There were dozens

of Monday morning meetings to analyze data about every aspect of the manufacturing process. There were job reviews. Two people were fired and two people were promoted. My expectations were clearly spelled out in individual and group meetings and they were put in writing. Some of the biggest gains came from improving the way we handled the work-in-process. I instituted process controls, changed some processes completely, and removed processes that were causing a higher failure rate. I bought some better error tracking software and calibration devices.

"Yikes! As the data cascades upon the hiring authority's bleeding ears the achievement is minimized if not forgotten. It is buried in an unhappy fog of details.

"There are reasons why data dumps occur. No one knows his achievements like the interviewee. He loves the details surrounding his accomplishments, but because he hasn't edited them he ends up sharing too many. It is mind numbing. Suddenly, after experiencing a few data dumps, the hiring authority doesn't want to hire this candidate for reasons he doesn't fully understand.

"The key is this. The central achievement in both the story and the data dump are identical, only the presentation style has changed. Can you see how style once again trumps substance?"

Julie said, "Yes. It's almost weird the way it works."

But My Job Is Nothing Special

"Stories can work well for anyone. About a year ago I worked pro bono for the Elam Davies Social Services Center in Chicago to help jobseekers develop interviewing skills.[10] They weren't your typical job-seeking group. They faced significant barriers such as a history of drug abuse, unstable housing, and inadequate insurance. This group included a person with HIV who was also in recovery

---

[10] The Elam Davies Social Services Center serves "the least, the last and the lonely" with dignity and respect and has done so since 1983. They are one of six programs operating within the Chicago Lights non-profit. If you are interested in learning more about them, then please visit www.chicagolights.org.

from drug addiction, and a few people who lacked teeth because they could not afford proper dental care. They were the poor, often forgotten people of 'slender means.'[11]

"When I offered to help them I wondered if I could. I knew these interviewing techniques worked well at the executive level, but wondered if they would work well at their level.

"It turns out they do. Stories highlighting the human condition— the struggles we all face—are moving whether they are set in the Mumbai slums of the hit movie, *Slumdog Millionaire,* or somewhere closer to home. The most menial activities can create a situational hook that grips the mind, charms the heart and stays with you long after.

"I still remember Sherry's story. Her job? Putting stickers on packages for a large retail chain. Her story? More compelling than you might first imagine:

> I started a job for a retail chain putting stickers on packages. The quota for each day was 1,000 and I was struggling at around 150. So were all of the other new-hires. About six of them quit after a day or two, but I don't quit. I saw someone who was overachieving her quota every day and asked her how she did it. After she showed me some of the tricks of the trade I not only made my quota, I was promoted to a higher level of responsibility.

Julie said, "That was touching."

"It is the power of stories. They make our smaller achievements seem bigger. In the case of Sherry's story, it opens with her struggling to overcome a production gap that seems insurmountable. New hires are giving up and hitting the exits in droves. It doesn't matter what your struggle may be, any triumph over difficult circumstances can communicate your worth to the

---

[11] I attended Rice University and its founder, William Marsh Rice, had a wonderful vision for this institution. It included granting access to an education at Rice University to the qualified students "of slender means." I was one of those students. Thanks Willie! (As he is fondly referred to at Rice.)

hiring authority.

"Like most stories, Sherry's is very versatile. It could be used to answer the following questions:

> Can you give me an example of how you have overcome adversity?
> What achievement are you proudest of?
> What are your strengths?

"When answering these questions she may need to modify her story by adding something at the end of it like, 'As this story shows, my strengths are persistence, hard work, learning quickly while on the job and problem solving. I say this because I was confronted with a difficult problem that many others couldn't solve, but I found a way to solve it.'

"This addition is like the moral of a story. Some stories have such an obvious message that no 'moral' is necessary. But unless a moral is overkill, adding one makes sense. The interviewer may already be exhausted when you interview, and his fried brain may fail to connect the dots."

Complex Sales and Stories

"Julie, do you remember when I told you the story about the woman who said she had been with me for two days and I had yet to try and sell her anything?"

"Yes. Are you trying to show me how stories are memorable?"

"That's an important, side benefit. But what I want you to see is how different the complex-sales approach is from the traditional-sales approach most interviewees use. When I first entered sales virtually every sales book espoused this traditional-sales model, and none of the ones I read ever advocated using stories. It was all about closing. Force the customer to decide to buy your product! But when I led a sales team in the complex-sales process we used stories to help sell our multi-million dollar systems, because they generate emotions that cause buying decisions. The pressure to buy our product came from inside the customer. They wanted to buy it, and they wanted to be associated with us. We were entertaining and weren't pushy.

"The secret of a story's interviewing power is the way it allows you to promote yourself in a way that doesn't seem pushy or boastful. The self-promotional aspects disappear in an entertaining story. It sells without seeming sales-y. Since people are happy to buy but hate being sold, this storytelling approach is essential to interviewing.

"And do you remember when I said that a focus on solutions made a sales presentation seem less like a sales presentation?"

"Yes, because you appear to be part of their team since they are also focused on solving their problems."

"You're a good listener. Stories sell without being sales-y because they show a hiring authority how you have overcome obstacles and solved problems that he has likely faced or now faces. Your story helps transform you into one of their team members who is focused on solving their problems."

Julie asked, "So how do you compose a good story?"

Entertaining By Design

Three Parts

"The key to writing a good story, and then telling it, is to follow a simple pattern. A story begins with a *situation* that attempts to hook the interest of the interviewer. For example, it can paint a seemingly hopeless situation that makes the listener want to know, 'How did he get out of that one?' or, 'What happens next?'

"The situation-stage is all about conflict. It introduces an obstacle that must be overcome. This obstacle is the villain of the story while you, the interviewee, are the hero.

"In the second phase we detail the *actions taken* to overcome the obstacle.

"The story ends with the *pay-off* or *result*. What was the impact of the actions taken?

"All three components of a story are important, but if you don't have a hook, you don't have a story. This is because the interviewer won't listen if a story doesn't interest him. But if you do hook the interviewer, then he will want to see how your situation was resolved."

Developing the Situational Hook

"This makes a strong hook a necessity, so start by locating your career's situational hooks. Think about the seemingly insurmountable obstacles you've faced and overcome. My interviewing story, for example, is one where the listener—in this case, you—wondered, 'How did he pull that one off.' It hooked your attention. I told it yesterday, but the hook was still set and today you still wanted to know how I out-interviewed someone who was so much more qualified. You may have forgotten the data, but not the story."

Julie said, "You're right. It's tough to argue against my own experience. You set the hook yesterday, and today I still vividly remember it. When I think about an interviewer being able to remember my story at the end of a long day, or the next day, I think, 'Wow! That's powerful.' "

"And we'll look at ways to reinforce the memory of these stories in just a minute.

"But returning to the subject of hooks. If you are finding it difficult to come up with hooks, then look over a list of standard interviewing questions, including behavioral questions, and answer them. Then see if your answer has a hook that can start a good story."

Julie looked puzzled. She asked, "What is a behavioral question? I may have been asked them before, and just don't know their name."

"They are questions that are becoming more and more popular. Here are a few examples:

> Give me an example of a goal you set, or were given, and how you achieved it.

> Give me an example of a mistake you made and how you

handled it.

Give me an example of a challenge you faced and how you dealt with it.

"Behavioral questions force the jobseeker to recount specific experiences or actions that show they have a sought after skill-set, or the character to handle adversity and succeed. Stories are very effective answers to these types of questions, because they can place these behaviors, or actions, in the most memorable and powerful format: a story.

"Are you ready for the next section?"

"Absolutely."

Actions Taken

"The *actions taken* segment needs to be guided by at least one of these rules. The actions:

1. Logically lead to the pay-off.

2. Add interest.

3. Make me look competent and trustworthy.

"In Bob's story the actions taken showed how he was an effective leader who led his team to make process improvements and go from being a demoralized group to a high-performance team.

"I'm going to read this actions taken section again, because I want you to note how these actions are concrete and directly tied to the pay-off that marks the conclusion of the story."

I then read:

> To turn this situation around I developed a plan with measurable milestones and whenever we achieved one we would have a mini-celebration. We focused on process improvements and began to build quality into the product.

"These actions logically lead to the pay-off. His celebrating successes strengthen his leadership image. His focus on process improvements shows how he knows what he is doing.

"A final word of advice on the actions taken section. Write down all of the important actions you took. There may be ten or more. Then pick the top three, or the ones that are necessary to lead to the pay-off, because too many details will overwhelm the mind."

The Pay-Off

"The story must produce a result that the hiring authority would value. Sometimes the pay-off is very short, as in the case of Sherry's story. Bob's pay-off section is much more detailed."

I read it once again:

> Before you knew it, we became a team and the quality gains we produced were dramatic. We reduced the failure rate five hundredfold. Instead of one error per 1,000 opportunities it became one per 500,000. This reduced the cost of manufactured goods by 10%. Margins improved for the first time in five years. The estimated annual impact was $200,000 to the bottom line. And our internal surveys showed my manufacturing team went from being among the least satisfied employees to being among the most satisfied in the company.

"What makes stories so powerful are the many emotions they can generate. For example, Bob's story has a feel-good, human-interest angle. A dysfunctional group, who the rest of the company probably viewed as losers, became a high-performance team. We tend to like or admire those people who make a difference in the lives of others.

"This story also inspires the emotion of hope, because it depicts an advanced leadership ability that might enable Bob to take a company to the next level. It inspires trust, because he shows he knows how to get the job done. It removes fear. Who would worry about their people reporting to him? All of these emotions are generated by one story and can help cause the hiring decision."

Money Is Emotion Quantified

"Bob's story also has a fair amount of facts and data which are typically boring to the interviewer unless they are about money. Money adds drama, because it is emotion quantified."

"What? What does that mean?" Julie asked.

"If you loan me $10 and I don't pay it back does this generate negative emotions?"

"Yes. I would probably think of you as being unreliable, or a sponge, and I'd probably never loan you another nickel."

"Think about that. A simple little sum of $10 generated the emotion of distrust and probably a little anger. Now what if you loaned me $1000 and I did not pay you back? Would the emotions be the same?"

"I get it. The answer is, 'No. I'd never speak to you again, because you cheated me out of a large sum of money.' "

"Here is another equation for you to remember, 'the more money, the more emotion, because…" I left the thought unfinished and allowed Julie to finish it.

"…Money is emotion quantified," she added.

"Righto. This makes money a different type of data. We need to include it in our interview answers. Most data and statistics will be forgotten, but a hiring authority will remember *added $200,000 to the bottom line* long after the interview is over.

"Money also gives scale and dimension to an accomplishment. Without providing the numbers, like the 10% reduction in the cost of manufactured goods and the $200,000 added to the bottom line, I leave the interviewer ignorant about the impact of my actions. By providing them I tell the interviewer, 'my productivity will make your company money.' "

The Unity of a Story

"Finally, all three sections of the story need to work. Imagine our manufacturing guy hooking his interviewer and telling him some of the positive things he did, and then ending with, 'This resulted in a 2% improvement in quality.'

"What do you think the interviewer's response to this story would be?"

"She might be disappointed or underwhelmed."

"I think you are spot on. A weak pay-off is a huge let down. The first two parts of the story created expectations that aren't being met by the conclusion. Stories with a weak pay-off will hurt you instead of help you. So if your story has a weak hook, or a less than strong ending, then throw it away."

Being Favorably Remembered

I then took this informal workshop on stories in a new direction by asking, "You've conducted interviews before, haven't you?"

Julie said, "Yes. Several times."

"So what happens after you finish the last interview of a long day; what's the next step?"

Julie thought about it and said, "I can remember sitting down and looking at the five resumes sitting in front of me and wondering, 'Who was this person or that person?' I found it hard to match their faces to their resumes."

"So how did you decide who to hire?"

"I don't remember. It's all kind of a big blur."

"Exactly. All of the candidates successfully performed a disappearing act. To keep from disappearing you need to use *repetition with variation*. Annoying commercials say the same thing many times, but we will say the same thing in different ways. For example, we can repeat the essence of our stories in the resume."

Embedded Stories

I handed Julie a sheet of paper. It showed how Bob's story about the five hundredfold improvement in quality could reappear in the resume:

- **Leadership:** Turned a demoralized group into a high-performance team with company leading job-satisfaction scores.

- **Quality:** Turned lowest quality product in industry into the highest, by reducing defect rate five hundredfold.

- **Bottom Line:** Lowered cost of manufactured goods 10% and added $200,000 to the bottom line.

"Now imagine this, Julie. The interviews are over and the interviewer looks through the stack of resumes and sees the above bullet points. They trigger the memory of the manufacturing manager's story and he thinks, 'Oh yeah, I remember that. What a great story. He inherited a demoralized group doing shoddy work and turned them into a group celebrating their success.' "

"Each remembered story separates you from the blur of the interviewing process. We want to be the high-definition image while our competitors are lost somewhere on a snowy screen."

Using Several Stories In an Interview

"How many stories you use will depend upon their power and their applicability. Would they capture the hiring authority's attention and imagination? Do they address the hiring authority's potential problems and needs? If they do, then why wouldn't you want to use such a story?"

"So how many stories do you use during one interview?" Julie asked.

I said, "At least six. Though I always had around ten stories ready."

"Ten!" Julie exclaimed, "Won't the interviewer begin to think, 'Oh no. Not another story!' "

"Not in my experience. If the stories are good and entertaining they will probably think, 'Oh good! He's got such great stories.'

"I think the secret to this process is keeping the stories short, about a minute in length. This means that during a fifty-minute interview only ten minutes, or twenty percent of my time, is spent answering questions with stories. The vast majority of the time is spent answering questions in a way I will outline shortly."

Where Storytellers Stumble

"If there is one area that jobseekers need to focus on prior to sharing their stories with a hiring authority it is this: editing. Stories are weak in the first-draft phase. In the next session we will go over the editing process."

Lessons

1. Stories have many advantages. They are entertaining, memorable and make achievements appear larger.

2. Stories begin with a situation that hooks the interviewer. No hook equals no story.

3. The actions taken should be concrete, lead to the pay-off and not overwhelm the interviewer with details.

4. The pay-off should be meaningful. If the situation and actions taken sections are strong, then the pay-off must be as well.

5. Money is emotion quantified. Detail cost-savings, revenue gains, etc., in dollars, whenever you can.

6. Develop 5-10 stories. None of them can be over two minutes in length and one minute is often better.

7. The Making of a Story

Deceptively Simple

"As you know, Julie, there are barriers to entry in business. If the barriers to entry are low, then there will be many competitors in that space. For example, nail shops that offer manicures and pedicures are everywhere, because the barriers to entering this business are low. But few companies manufacture rockets capable of reaching the space station, because the barriers to entry are high.

"One of the beauties of using stories is the way the barrier to entry is higher than most people expect. Few take the time, or exert the effort to write, edit and remember a good story."

Julie said, "The stories you told me seemed simple and easy enough."

"That's where most people stumble. They equate simple with easy. I'd like to share with you a paragraph written by a great prose stylist. It shows how difficult writing is. His name is William Zinsser, and the paragraph comes from his book, *On Writing Well*. This is his description of a reader who is struggling to understand something that is poorly written."

Creative Writing: Behind the Curtain

I read aloud:

Faced with such a variety of obstacles, the reader is at first a remarkably tenacious bird. He tends to blame himself. He obviously missed something, he thinks, and he goes back over the mystifying sentence, or over the whole paragraph, piecing it out like an ancient rune, making guesses and moving on. But he won't do this for long. He will soon run out of patience. The writer is making him work too hard— harder than he should have to work—and the reader will look for a writer who is better at his craft.[12]

I looked up and asked, "What do you think of the quality of his writing?"

"It seems to be just fine," Julie answered.

"I would agree. As he notes in his book, this paragraph was the result of being rewritten four or five times. Now look at this sheet. This was his final rewrite. Don't read it, because I'll hand you a corrected version that's easier to read. Just note the number of changes, particularly the number of words he deletes."

I handed her a page detailing his many revisions:

Faced with [these] ~~such a variety of~~ obstacles, the reader is at first a remarkably tenacious bird. He ~~tends to~~ blame[s] himself[--]~~H~~ he obviously missed something, ~~he thinks,~~ and he goes back over the mystifying sentence, or over the whole paragraph, piecing it out like an ancient rune, making guesses and moving on. But he won't do this for long. ~~He will soon run out of patience.~~ The writer is making him work too hard ~~—harder than he should have to work~~—and the reader will look for ~~a writer~~ [one] who is

---

[12] William Zinsser, *On Writing Well: An Informal Guide to Writing Non-Fiction* (New York: Harper & Row, Publishers, Inc., 1985), pp. 10-11. Please note that this quotation is slightly changed from the original as it appears in the book. The book has an image of two typewritten manuscript pages with his handwritten editing notes on them. I am sharing his fourth or fifth draft without corrections in this quote. The quotation that follows will show *typewritten* corrections, followed by the final draft as it appears in the book.

better at his craft.[13]

I then said, "He has so many edits on this final draft that it looks like he was working from a first draft instead of his fourth or fifth. And he was a superb writer!

"Now here is the final corrected copy. They make the final draft lean and clean, which is what you aim for."

I handed her a final sheet so that she could read it without all of the notations:

> Faced with these obstacles, the reader is at first a remarkably tenacious bird. He blames himself—he obviously missed something, and he goes back over the mystifying sentence, or over the whole paragraph, piecing it out like an ancient rune, making guesses and moving on. But he won't do this for long. The writer is making him work too hard, and the reader will look for one who is better at his craft.[14]

The Hard Work of Writing Well

Julie looked up and said, "I thought writing for these professional writers was a lot easier than this. I had no idea."

"When I first read this some time ago, it was a revelation. Editing is a lot of work. And it is necessary, because writing well is difficult. Zinsser noted this even as he shared some of his editing practices."

I then read the following from his book *On Writing Well*:

> With each rewrite I try to make what I have written tighter, stronger and more precise, eliminating every element that is not doing useful work. Then I go over it once more, reading it aloud, and am always amazed at how much clutter can still be cut.
>
> …Writing is hard work. A clear sentence is no accident. Very few sentences come out right the first time, or even

---

[13] Zinsser, pp. 10-11.
[14] Zinsser, p. 12.

the third time. ...If you find that writing is hard, it's because it is hard. It is one of the hardest things that people do.[15]

"In other words, writing an effective story takes time, effort and determination. Most of your competitors for a job opportunity will not invest the time or effort. They fail to see how preparing for an interview is similar to an athlete's preparation for a race. If you don't prepare, then you can't compete with those who do.

"Are you ready?"

"I was born ready."

The First Draft

I liked Julie's spunk. I then handed her a sheet of paper and said, "This is the first draft of a story. It's about an achievement I could highlight during an interview. It's not terrible, but it needs work. As Zinsser wrote, 'Very few sentences come out right the first time, or even the third time.' "

On the sheet in Julie's hand was the following first draft:

Situational Hook

I had a Region Manager who was being thrown out of hospitals and not allowed to return. He was losing established, large accounts. He was also posting declining numbers. He was nearing retirement, but I was given the authority to terminate his employment. I did not want to do this for a variety of reasons so I elected to make him a sales-performance-coaching candidate.

Actions Taken

I traveled with him to see what he was doing that was making people so angry they banned him from entering their account, and I noticed how he was unconsciously responding to a customer's legitimate questions in a belittling way. So I brought this to his attention, modeled

---

[15] Zinsser, pp. 11, 12.

some more effective approaches to answering questions and I never witnessed this problem, or even heard of it surfacing, again.

The next step was to teach him the art of differentiation, or comparing the competitor's product to yours in a way that favors your product and is inoffensive. I showed him a differentiation presentation I used, went over it with him, and then he added these slides to his presentation. The very next day he closed a big sale and differentiated perfectly.

Pay-Off

Within two years his numbers had improved to the point where he became our Region Manager of the Year.

Assessment

"When we create our first draft we cannot pronounce, 'It is good,' because it is not. It is fat with empty words and unnecessary phrases. So the next step is to cut the first draft's number of words in half. We want our final draft to be lean and muscular. It gives our story energy.

"The first question we ask is, 'Does the first paragraph set the hook with a difficult situation? Does it?"

Julie answered, "It's not too bad. It makes me want to find out what happens to Joe."

"So what we have is a hook that needs strengthening. One of its weaknesses is the way it meanders toward its objective. But after five editing passes I was able to reduce the number of words by more than 50%. Let's see if this makes the situation clearer."

Situation

I took out another sheet with the edited story and then read the situational hook out loud:

I had a Region Manager who was losing large accounts, posting declining numbers, and being banned from hospitals. I was faced with either turning him around or firing him.

"Can you see how removing the clutter makes this situation clearer? We don't want the interviewer to struggle to understand our story, because it weakens its impact.

"Also, note how a clear story has more energy than a cluttered one. Instead of plodding, it races toward its objective. The pace becomes livelier."

Actions Taken

"The second section was filled with verbal clutter. Its removal improved the story dramatically."

I then read the edited *actions taken* section:

> So I travelled with him and found out why he was being banned from hospitals. On two occasions he belittled the questions customers asked and was unaware he was doing so. This problem stopped after coaching him.

> I then showed him how to differentiate our product and added these slides to his presentation. The next day he differentiated perfectly and closed a big sale.

"The first draft of the actions taken was 128 words. It is now 64 words. This process illustrates why we must write down our stories and edit them several times. Because when we tell a story off the top of our heads we ramble on like a bad first draft. The power of our story drowns in a flood of useless words.

"These two sentences give you a sense of editing's impact."

I read the following:

First Draft

So I brought this to his attention, modeled some more effective approaches to answering questions and I never witnessed this problem, or even heard of it surfacing, again.

Final Draft

This problem stopped after coaching him.

"Wow!" Julie said, "Your first draft was really lame."

"Yes, and you can bet yours will be too. That's why we edit them several times, because if we don't our stories will be tedious."

Pay-Off

"The final section..." Julie interrupted me and said, "The last section is my favorite part of the entire story..."

I returned the favor and interrupted her, "I know, because it's the shortest. Well you will now like it even more, because I made it much shorter. It goes from, 'Within two years his numbers had improved to the point where he became our Region Manager of the Year.' To, 'Two years later he was Region Manager of the Year.'

"This shortest of sections goes from nineteen words to ten. Is it necessary to say, 'his numbers had improved to the point'? Would he be getting Region Manager of the Year if his numbers declined? Superfluous words delay getting to the point."

The Final Step

"The final step involves adding details that give our story a greater emotional impact. We humanize it. We want the interviewer to care about Joe's fate to make the pay-off more satisfying.

"Here's one more sheet of paper. The added emotional elements are in bold print."

I handed Julie a sheet with the following text:

> **Joe was the best-liked Region Manager on my team. He was funny, kind, and nearing retirement.** He was also losing large accounts, posting declining numbers, and being banned from hospitals. I was faced with either turning him around or firing him.
>
> So I travelled with him and found out why he was being banned from hospitals. On two occasions he belittled the questions customers asked and was unaware he was doing so. **This was completely out of character, and** this problem stopped after coaching him.

I then showed him how to differentiate our product and added these slides to his presentation. **Differentiation was a key to our success, but it is not an easy skill to master. After only one class Joe said he thought he could do it without my help.** The next day he differentiated perfectly and closed a big sale.

Two years later he was Region Manager of the Year. **When Joe received this award he got a standing ovation from the entire company.**

Julie looked up and said, "The achievement is good by itself, but in the story format it seems bigger. But what I really like is the way a story seems so natural. It doesn't seem like you're selling anyone."

"Stories offer a solution to the problem of interviewing. We are asked to boast about our achievements in an interview, but people don't like boasting. Stories enable us to promote ourselves in a way that doesn't seem like boasting.

"Now one of the reasons we had a session on responsibility and no excuses is this: Stories will take work, but they are worth the work. If you have zero tolerance for excuses, you will put in the hard work to write, edit, edit, edit and remember these stories."

Julie said, "Don't worry about me. I'll put in the time. I'm tired of finishing second. I want a medal for my efforts."

"Excellent! Since our time before your next interview is limited I want you to work on writing three stories this evening. Edit them and bring them to me tomorrow. We can then do some final edits together."

"They will be awful."

"Not when we're finished with them."

Lessons

1. Speaking off the top of one's head is like a first draft—full of unnecessary words and sentences that ramble.

2. Our stories must be written down so that we can edit them.

3. Good writing is hard work. It is a barrier to entry because

few will invest the time and effort to gain this advantage.

4. First drafts are cut in half, when possible, and then emotionally powerful details are added.

8. Scripted or Unscripted Answers?

The Interview's Dominant Behavior

Julie and I met the next day and she seemed different. Yesterday she was a skeptic who used sarcasm to keep her distance, and today she was a student who bought into the program.

I asked her, "How are your stories coming along?"

"Zinsser was right. Writing is hard."

"Hang in there. We'll go over them in just a bit. But first, I've got some good news and bad news. Which do you want first?"

"I think I'll start with the good news."

"Okay. Today I will be sharing with you more techniques that will make it easier for you to finish first in the job interview."

"That's good news. Now for the bad…"

"It involves more writing and editing."

"What? C'mon! I don't want to become an author. I just want a job."

"And I want to help you get one. So let me ask you a question. What simple communication process dominates the interview?"

Julie said, "The interviewer asks questions and the interviewee answers them."

"Correct. It is a simple process called Q & A. It makes your answers one of the most important behaviors in an interview. Now here's another question."

"Shoot."

"Which answer to a question will be stronger: The first answer that pops into your head, or the answer that was written down, edited several times, and is crystal clear and succinct?"

"Since I've seen what editing does to a story I'd have to say the scripted, thoroughly edited answer is stronger."

"Much stronger. If someone asks me what my strengths are I may give the following wordy, clumsy answer:

> I think my integrity is a great strength. It's a quality that affects everything. It helps you build and sustain trust with others. So it is the key to developing strong relationships. And along with integrity I'd have to add leadership ability. If you were to ask my last boss what one of my biggest strengths was I'm pretty sure he'd say, 'Leadership.'

"That answer is not an interviewing crime, but it's flat. The way it gropes toward an answer makes this jobseeker look lost and lacking competence. As answers of this sort continue an uneasy feeling begins to grow in the interviewer.

"Here's a more effective answer. It's scripted and it doesn't lose its way."

> My greatest strength? The way I combine management and leadership skills. Leaders see where their team needs to go to be successful and they have a clear vision of how to get there. I used these skills to develop a comprehensive plan to turn my unproductive group into a high-performance team. But I couldn't have achieved this goal without strong managerial skills like delegating and coaching. For example, to show them I trusted them I started delegating projects that required them to learn new skills. Then I

would coach them until they acquired them. They began to see how I wouldn't let them fail and they began to trust me. In a few months we began to function as a team and our productivity increased dramatically. So I would say my greatest strength is the way I combine excellent management and leadership skills.

"Julie, this answer went through many rewrites. My first attempt at answering it was slightly garbled and confused. But during an interview it's even more difficult to give a clear answer off the top of our head because of the pressure.

"Since many of the same questions are asked by every interviewer, it helps to have scripted, edited, well-rehearsed answers to the top twenty questions or so."

Objection

Julie's brief flirtation with being an accepting student intent on learning from her teacher came to a screeching halt. She said, "The problem with your approach is this: It will seem scripted and people will sense that you are not real, you're just rehearsed and inauthentic."

"Welcome back, Julie! I thought the old you must have gone away on vacation or something. You could at least have added 'robotic, fake and nauseating.' "

"Next time, but for now I am trying to be a kinder, gentler Julie."

"You are funny. But you do bring up a valid concern that I once had. It vanished after I developed and delivered a training class. In this class I thoroughly edited, rehearsed and memorized virtually every line of every slide. I was as scripted as possible. I was also anonymously graded by each student on the value of the information and my presentation style. So were the other instructors. In every class I finished first among the instructors in both content and delivery, except for one where I finished second by the narrowest of margins. And in the comments sections the students never accused me of being wooden, scripted, or robotic.

"What happened was the exact opposite. Their comments indicated

I was dynamic, persuasive and captivating. I quickly learned that the audience is impressed by the vitality of our presentation when we speak in muscular sentences stripped of fat.

"There is another huge benefit to rehearsing a script to the point of memorizing it. Do you know what that is?"

"No, but I'm captivated."

Rehearsing

"Then I will hurry while you're still under my spell. Rehearsing allows you to relax and enjoy the interview. You are like a person who has trained for a great performance and delivers one with confidence.

"Then, as you answer questions succinctly and powerfully, your interviewing competence inspires the emotion of trust. Your relaxed demeanor and occasional smiles give the impression that you are comfortable, and the emotional tuning fork who is interviewing you begins to feel comfortable as well. Fears about making a bad hire start to recede when the interviewer considers you for the job."

Final Remarks

"Let's say that you've prepared twenty answers to twenty typical questions, and the hiring authority only asks two of them. Has your time been wasted?"

Julie's answer surprised me, "No. This process forces you to think about what you've done, and express it clearly. I bet scripted answers have the same flexibility as stories. One answer can be used to answer a variety of questions. But if they go unused, I am still articulate about what I've done."

"Julie, you are a fast learner. The funny thing about scripting answers is this: Nobody objects to scripting an answer for the question, 'Would you tell me about yourself?' Almost everyone tells you to work on this answer in advance, and I am in complete agreement.

"But if scripting an answer in advance works for, 'Tell me about yourself,' then wouldn't it work for other questions? And if not, then why not?"

Julie conceded, "That's a good point." Then she came up with a possible problem with this approach, "But could this approach cause people to over prepare? There is a point where too much work can make you tense, or it can lead to diminishing returns."

"The diminishing returns can be a real problem, but not if you are working with a coach. The challenge, accountability, and creative conflict keep the work fresh and energizing.

"As for too much preparation, that becomes a problem when you try and cram it all in at the last minute. That's one of the reasons why you and I will only be preparing in a few areas for your upcoming interview. We won't have enough time to do everything, but we will have time to make a difference.

"Now we will script an answer to 'tell me about yourself,' and show how you can use repetition with variation to make this answer even more powerful."

Lessons

1. Our answers to likely questions become clearer and stronger when we thoroughly edit a scripted response.

2. Memorizing these answers do not result in the jobseeker looking scripted. It leads to the confident presentation of skillfully crafted solutions.

3. The energy of uncluttered answers makes the jobseeker look dynamic and intentional, not meandering and lost.

4. If behaviors cause perceptions that cause emotions that cause hiring decisions, and the number one behavior on display is answers to questions, then strengthening this behavior's influence is essential.

9. The Value Statement

Scripted? How About Three Scripts

"Julie, in your last interview were you asked the 'tell me about yourself' question?"

"Yes. I always get asked that question."

"So how much time did you spend answering it?"

"Too much time I think."

"Why?"

"Well I developed three possible answers to this question, and after I gave the first one I thought, 'Maybe I should give the second one too.' And then…"

"You didn't."

"Yes. I gave the third one too. I think I was trying too hard."

"No question. But you were also being true to yourself. Analytical types tend to pursue additional information, and sometimes they share too much as well. They value information and assume others do to the same degree. Does that sound like you?"

Julie bowed her head and said, "Guilty as charged, your honor."

"You're not alone. Even non-analytical types tend to drone on when answering this question. If ever there was a case for scripting, this is it.

"A key to answering this question is keeping it short. Make it two minutes or less. My answer is typically kept closer to one minute. It helps highlight the way my competitors drone on endlessly."

"But what if they come back to you and say, 'I just asked you to tell me about yourself and is that all you've got to say?' What do you say then?" Julie asked.

"The way I end my answer to this question doesn't allow them to respond that way."

"What? How can it possibly do that?"

To which I answered, "Before we talk about how I end this answer, let's look at how I start it."

We Begin With Education

"Most people who answer this question offer a confusing picture of what they've done and who they are. It's a massive download of information. Some of it's interesting and relevant, but taken as a whole it is forgettable for the most part.

"This format attempts to present a clear picture by tying everything together. It doesn't just start with our educational experience because this is expected; no, it starts with education because it is the logical place to begin. After all, our achievements and skill sets logically extend from what we've learned, just as theory typically precedes practice.

"A value statement for Bob, my manufacturing example, might start as follows:

> I went to Prestigious University and graduated with a degree in business. I've also graduated from training courses in lean manufacturing and am a six-sigma black belt. My education continued at Acme, Inc., a Fortune 100 company, where I spent ten years learning invaluable teambuilding, management and leadership skills. I also worked at Badda Bing, LLC, an entrepreneurial startup. It allowed me to be creative and design entirely new

approaches to manufacturing for this company.

"With that we are finished with the first section of our answer. It starts the story about yourself with the education you've received from several sources: school, seminars and work. The important thing is to highlight educational experiences that are directly tied to the achievements and skill sets you will be mentioning next.

Repetition With Variation

"It works like this, 'My education taught me about teambuilding, I have achieved teambuilding success in the corporate arena as the following example shows, and one of my many skill sets is....' "

"Teambuilding," Julie blurted out, finishing my sentence before I could. She added, "I know. I have psychic gifts."

"Extraordinary. Anyway, this is another way of using repetition with variation to make your message memorable, because that is one of our most important goals. And here is what is unusual. Our manufacturer will beat this teambuilding drum three times in his one minute value statement, and yet it will not seem like overkill."

Julie asked another good question, "Perhaps not, but isn't this approach guilty of educational overkill? Won't I fare better by spending more time on my achievements and skill sets?"

"I won't answer *yes* or *no* to that question. Experiment and tailor your answer to fit you and the image you are trying to create in the mind of the interviewer. But from my perspective I am trying to differentiate myself from my competition by doing the following: Answering this tired question in a new and compelling way. Who answers this question by turning their work experience into an educational experience? Probably no one, ever, in the interviewer's experience. And I am also trying to communicate this idea: I've never stopped learning and every job I've had has been a valuable learning experience.

Wide-Ranging but Brief

"Finally, with the two companies I've chosen, one massive and the other small, I'm trying to communicate how I've learned to work and thrive in very different settings. Big companies say they want to be more entrepreneurial, but they fear hiring people from small companies because they may not be able to adapt to the more structured approach of their larger organization. I want to let them know I bring entrepreneurial skills with a big corporation pedigree.

"But don't reference more than two companies in this first section, because we want to keep this answer short. About one minute in duration. This is another way of differentiating yourself from your competitors who tend to dredge the bottom of their subconscious mind to give every little detail about every company they've worked for. By the time their answer reaches the three-minute mark their likability rating begins to plummet.

"Julie, when a person drones on about themselves at a party do we like to sit there and listen?"

"No. We want to turn around and walk away, but we are trapped, compelled to listen because of our manners."

"Indeed. And why would we expect an interviewer to all of the sudden develop a taste for a complete stranger droning on about themselves for five minutes? They hate it. So we try and keep this answer short."

Why Is This Simple Question so Tough?

I then took the conversation in a slightly different direction, "Do you remember how you struggled with this question?"

"Yes. And I struggle with it every time even though I'm always prepared for it. Why is that?"

"Because this question forces you to sell the most difficult product: yourself. It is not a natural thing to do, so it's easy to see why you don't feel good about your answer.

"Since this question forces you to sell yourself, and people don't like to be sold, keep it short."

Julie said, "I'm happy to do so. This question usually appears at the beginning of the interview. It seems to generate negative momentum. So how do we package the rest of the answer? I'm tired of struggling with it."

Achievements

"The next stage involves talking about your achievements in a way that communicates your value to an organization, without trying to list most of your achievements. We want to keep the answer short and avoid data-dumping.

"Bob, our manufacturing example, could say something like this about his achievements:

> My education led to the many achievements I've included on my resume. But one that I would like to highlight is the way I used my leadership skills to turn a demoralized group into a high-performance team and used my advanced manufacturing training to locate quality problems and fix them. This improved product quality five hundredfold and reduced the cost of goods sold by 10%. It also added $200,000 to the bottom line.

Julie spotted a potential problem with this answer and asked, "But this five hundredfold increase in quality is a data-point. Why mention that when it is presented better in a story format?"

"Trust me, Julie, I would find a way to work my story into this interview."

Julie continued, "But since you're repeating this five hundredfold improvement, haven't you diminished the story's impact? Now it won't be a surprising result."

"The impact is actually enhanced by repetition, because it helps the interviewer remember what you've told him. I would change the story slightly by prefacing the pay-off section with: 'Those were the actions I took to produce the five hundredfold reduction in errors, and the $200,000 to the bottom line that I mentioned before.'

"Are you ready for the conclusion?"

"Only if you show me how you prevent the hiring authority from asking you why your answer is so short."

"You've got a deal."

Skill Sets

"I think you will like the way this answer ends because it gives this answer something it almost never has: energy. We achieve this by rattling off our most important skill sets at the end of the answer, and then we add a question that has literally made hiring authorities smile."

I then read:

> I'm a strong leader and an excellent follower. But if there is anything that sets me apart from others it is probably this: I love what I do and this helps me bring an infectious, teambuilding enthusiasm to the job. I'm also a disciplined manager, an observant coach, a creative problem-solver, an effective team builder and a determined producer of results.
>
> Which of these areas would you like to discuss?

Julie smiled. She saw how this concluding question prevented the hiring authority from asking, "Is that it?"

I continued, "This answer covers a lot of ground quickly. It took Bob about one minute to answer this question, but in this short amount of time he showed how he possessed the must-have qualifications of leadership and management abilities, how he picked up valuable skills from both small and large companies, how he produced results, and he was still able to use repetition with variation to make his message more memorable."

Differentiation

"It also utilized a very powerful sales tool: differentiation. Do you remember how I mentioned it in the story on coaching?"

"Yes and you just mentioned it again. So what is this process?" Julie looked down and said, "I can't believe I'm asking a question about how to sell?"

"It's okay, Julie, think of it as a persuasion tool and not a sales tool."

"Thanks. Persuasion sounds better to me."

"I thought it might. Differentiation is illustrating how you are different from your competitors in a way that favors you. For example, Bob, our manufacturer, told the interviewer his love for manufacturing is what probably made him different from other candidates. To say you love what you do is a strong statement, and one that other candidates might not say. Therefore, it makes you different in a favorable way. And Bob helps to highlight this difference by saying, '…if there is anything that sets me apart from others it is probably this.'

"Another way to differentiate yourself is to determine what your greatest strength is and then make a statement like, 'If there is one thing that seems to be critical to succeeding in this position it is…' and then spend a good amount of interviewing time showing how you possess this strength in abundance.

"What you are trying to do is reposition the debate in a way that favors you. It's like choosing the best terrain on the battlefield. In other words, if your competitors have to compete against you on this ground, then they will likely be at a severe disadvantage. Better yet, this strong skill-set will appear even stronger because of your stories.

"Here is how I used differentiation. When I was interviewing for the position to lead a sales team in the launch of a revolutionary product I told the hiring authority, 'I think the most important qualification for this job is having had experience launching a revolutionary product. Unless you've done it before you won't understand how critical it is to be passionate about your product, or how to express this passion in a way that lights a fire in the hearts of the early adopters.' And I continued to emphasize this differentiating skill-set.

"I wanted to reposition the opportunity onto favorable ground. I had launched a revolutionary product before and it was likely that my competitors had not."

Trust

"Did you note how he also took a trust-building step by

accentuating how he was also a good follower?"

Julie said, "Yeah, I noticed," as she fidgeted in her chair. "Look, I like the value-statement format, but this stuff about being an excellent follower…it just seems like you are kissing up to your future boss. Won't he disrespect you for this?"

"No, because it addresses an area of potential concern. Bob made the case that he is a very strong leader. His people follow him. Sometimes strong leaders don't like being led, or act like they're the boss, and to hire such a person could cause the hiring authority an enormous headache. Any concerns our strengths create should be eliminated, because it may be the most emotionally powerful issue to this interviewer."

Repetition With Variation in the Resume

"You've delivered a memorably different value statement and the hiring authority, who just finished his long day of interviewing, looks over the resumes and reads your Summary of Qualifications. There he finds a synopsis of your value statement and the memory-enhancing power of repetition with variation lifts you out of the blur afflicting the other candidates."

I handed Julie another sheet of paper and read from my copy:

> *A senior executive offering over 10 years of manufacturing experience with Fortune 100 companies and smaller technology-based startups. A passionate leader who builds highly motivated teams that have delivered five hundredfold quality gains and hundreds of thousands of dollars to the bottom line. A creative problem-solver, observant coach and disciplined manager.*

After Julie finished reading this I continued, "As the hiring authority finishes reading this summary he may think, 'I remember this guy. I loved his elevator speech. It was so different.' As he scans the resume the bullet points remind him of Bob's stories. While other resumes go to the bottom of the pile, his goes to the top."

Julie said, "Your answer is so much better than mine was. You

89

keep it short, you focus on repeating the most important themes, and I love the ending."

"Style trumps substance. We laid the foundation and now we're building on it." I said and thought, "Soon she will be performing at a much higher level."

The Assignment

Julie said, "My head is about to explode."

I smiled and said, "My objective from the very beginning was to blow your mind."

"Yes, and the pieces keep getting smaller and smaller."

"Okay. We are finished for today, because I have an assignment for you. I want you to develop a script, no longer than two minutes, that follows the format I've just given you. Sound good?"

"Sounds good."

"Excellent. Tomorrow we'll go over your value statement and then cover another critical topic: suicide questions."

Julie gave me one of her patented looks and asked, "Did you give these questions that name?"

"I did."

"How could I have guessed?"

Lessons

1. The Value Statement is the answer to the most-asked interview question: tell me about yourself.

2. It has four parts: Education, achievements, skill sets and a closing question.

3. Keep it less than two minutes and repeat important themes.

4. The gist of this statement becomes the Summary of Qualifications on your resume.

10. Suicide and Showcase Questions

I asked Julie, "Wouldn't it be great if you knew the questions the interviewer was going to ask before he asked them?"

She replied, "We kind of do, don't we? Aren't all of the typical questions posted on a hundred different websites?"

"Right you are," I said, "And guess who visits these websites about one hour before the interviewing begins?"

"The hiring authority."

"Yes, many of them do, though some do a much better job of preparing for an interview than others.

"Now, since scripted answers are more powerful, we need to script answers for those nasty questions that invite you to commit suicide."

Julie said, "I think I've been asked a question like that. After I answered one I thought, 'I didn't just say that, did I?' "

"Exactly," I replied. "Suicide questions are like land mines. Step on them and your chance of being hired can blow up. We'll look at some of the ones that come up most frequently.

Suicide Questions

Julie asked, "Don't you just hate these questions?"

"No. I love suicide questions and look forward to them."

"Why am I not surprised?"

"And you will too. They are another way for you to separate yourself from the crowd. While the answers of others range from DOA to OK, your answer will make the interviewer think, 'That may be the best answer to that question that I've ever heard.'

"The first question we will look at it is the oldie-goldie of the suicide question category,

'What are your weaknesses?' "

Julie then said, "Here's what I hate about that question. It's like the little voyeur across the table is asking me to expose myself."

"Yes, the weakness question is an attempt to get you to open your kimono and to commit interviewing suicide. But we don't accept the invitation because rule number one in answering suicide questions is: *We will keep our liabilities concealed.* The best image I can offer is an iceberg. The majority of its mass is underwater and kept from view.

"Everyone has liabilities, but to freely share yours in a forthright manner is to commit interviewing suicide. Our liabilities generate negative emotions like fear. Negative emotions are interviewing poison, so we need to keep our liabilities beneath the surface.

"And the second rule is: *Surround your weaknesses with strengths.*"

Julie asked, "What does that mean?"

"When asked to reveal a weakness start your answer with a strength, offer a weakness that is not job-disqualifying, and finish your answer with another strength. This minimizes the emotional impact of the weakness by taking advantage of two well-known psychological processes: the primacy and recency effects.

"What is said first and what is said last is more memorable than what is said in the middle. So we put our well-tailored liability in the forgettable middle so that our strengths are remembered and not our weaknesses.

"The interviewer is asking us to violate a fundamental interviewing principle. We are to always be positive and these liability questions ask us to be negative about ourselves. So we remove the negative impact of our answer to this question by bracketing it with positive strengths."

Dishonest? Manipulative?

You could always tell when a subject made Julie uncomfortable. She would begin to squirm, as if invisible ants were crawling up her legs. So I gently asked, "Is there something you'd like to discuss?"

"Yes there is," she said, "Isn't this dishonest? If they ask, 'What are your biggest weaknesses?' and I tell them something other than my biggest weakness, then aren't I lying?"

"An excellent question, and a difficult one to answer, but I'll try. Certain social settings require filtering information in a way that is both expected and appreciated. When you are asked at a dinner party, 'How are you doing?' Do you say, 'I'm in the deepest pit of hell. This past year has been so awful that I've contemplated suicide for the first time.'

"Even if this is true, you don't say it. Instead you answer, 'I'm fine. How are you?' because the social conventions of a dinner party demand a sunny, positive response. It's a time of entertainment, not a therapy session.

"Truth is also on a holiday at funerals, and this is also expected and appreciated. At a memorial service for an abusive, vile, reptile of a person you will hear those who were abused praising this person. They do this because funerals are about honoring the departed, and not about sharing the unvarnished, upsetting truth.

"The interview is another social setting where no one expects you to share the unvarnished truth about your weaknesses. In fact, the hiring authority would be furious if everyone did. Imagine flying in four candidates for interviews and having every one of them disqualify themselves.

"Here is what is expected of you. During an interview you are expected to present yourself in the best possible light. To do otherwise is to waste the interviewer's time and show how little you understand about this process.

"Are you okay with that answer?"

Julie shook her head up and down and then shook it from side to side and said, "Kind of yes and kind of no."

"Normally I'd say you just gave me a weak, non-answer, but in this case I think your answer's correct. The interview is a flawed process where flawed and irrational hiring authorities get to make irrational choices based on what they see and hear from flawed and irrational people. It's a slice of life. A lot messier than we'd like it to be."

Answering Suicide Questions

What Is Your Greatest Weakness?

"What is your *greatest* weakness? There are many ways to answer this question. You can pick a weakness that involves a skill that is not required for the job. For example, you might answer:

> I am very strong in my communication abilities, but I'm not that good at public speaking. It's probably a weakness because I just don't like doing it. But when you take away the podium I am very comfortable communicating with large groups of colleagues, or people I might be managing.

"This weakness was not essential to his job and it was sandwiched between two statements emphasizing strong communication skills."

Julie was still troubled about this and said, "Look, public speaking is not anyone's greatest weakness!"

To which I replied, "How do you know? Who is to judge what our greatest weakness is? With all of our biases, are we the perfect judge? Is the interviewer the one who can tell us what our greatest weakness is?

"Another strategy is to place the weakness in the past:

> I'm a very decisive person and I know where I am going.
> So earlier in my career I would sometimes formulate
> directions for my team without seeking any of their
> feedback. This can hurt the development of a team. So now
> I actively seek my team's feedback and get their buy-in
> before setting off in a new direction. Since I put this
> process in place I've gotten consistent, strong results from
> my team.

"In this answer we began with a strength—decisiveness. We then
moved into how this strength caused management and leadership
problems in the past. But now the problem is under control and it's
become a significant strength.

Julie asked, "What if the interviewer says, 'I asked for your
weakness and you've given me something that sounds more like a
strength. Are you saying you have no weaknesses?' "

"I'd answer, 'I wish that was the case, but it's not. My being too
decisive is both a genuine strength and a genuine weakness. My
preferred path is to decide, whether I have the team's feedback or
not. Now, on rare occasions, I still forget to ask for it. So it's a bit
of a struggle to keep seeking their input. But it has been getting
easier to do this, because I get such positive reinforcement from
the results this approach delivers.' "

I then asked Julie, "How was that?"

"Okay. So what you are saying is you don't back down when they
challenge you?"

"Heavens no! That would make me appear deceptive, like I can't
keep my story straight. Since every strength has a weakness, why
would I back down from what is self-evident?"

The Best Answer: Using MBTI®

"Now this next answer is probably the best because it reveals a
level of understanding that most candidates do not possess. It also
bases the weakness on objective analysis. It ends up making you

look far stronger than before the question was asked:

> I think it's hard to admit weaknesses or even understand what they might be. So I turned to the Myers-Briggs Type Indicator® to get some objective insights into my strengths and weaknesses.
>
> It told me one of my greatest strengths was the ability to take in large amounts of information, see patterns others don't see, develop creative solutions, and then have the tenacity to implement them.
>
> But all types have blind spots or potential weaknesses. According to Myers-Briggs a potential blind spot for my type can be failing to consider the impact of my decisions on the individuals in my team. And this used to happen often before I knew about this blind spot. So I developed a leadership team from among my direct reports and they review those plans that will impact the entire team before they're implemented. In almost every case this resulted in improving my plan. And, just as important, there is greater buy-in because my team knows I've listened to their input.

"The beauty of this answer is that while it reveals a genuine, objectively-determined weakness, it also shows a much greater strength, a degree of emotional intelligence that the other candidates are unlikely to express. And did you notice how this weakness evaporates like the morning dew when it's sandwiched between two strengths?"

"Yes. I'm trying to remember what your weakness was and you just told me."

"Exactly. But the important thing is you must admit a weakness. To not do so suggests you have an arrogance that's almost pathological. So answer this question in a way that helps your cause."

Julie said, "I'm new to Myers-Briggs. Do you think it's helpful to learn this system for interviewing?"

"Absolutely. We'll cover it in some detail later on, because this is something I want to work with you on. But it may be too much for you to work on before your upcoming interview. You've already got a lot of prep-work on your plate. After I give you some material on using Myers-Briggs in an interview, you can decide whether or not it is too much work colliding with too little time."

"But if I can't jam it in before my interview, then why would I need to study it later on?"

"You can use it during the second round of interviews and the time-lag in between the first and second round should provide you with more than enough time. Besides, the uses of Myers-Briggs aren't limited to interviewing. I use in my consulting practice to assist in the development of leaders, teams, conflict resolution, and on and on."[16]

Julie then asked, "Are there other suicide risks I need to be aware of?"

"Yes. Interviewers are very fond of them." I then unearthed another potential land mine:

"Who was your best boss and who was your worst?"

Julie said, "I can honestly say I hate that question too."

I laughed and replied, "Yes, but you have to learn to love these questions. While you are dancing through the minefield and your competitors are not, then guess who finishes first?"

"Point taken. This interviewing world reminds me of *Through the Looking Glass*. What's up is down and what's right is left."

"Exactly. And that's why most people are running in the wrong direction. The wrong direction looks right.

"Now, since we must always be positive and limit the exposure of liabilities, your answer to this question might be, 'Thankfully, all of my bosses were great teachers who've helped me improve. But if I were to rank order them I would say John Doe was my best and Joe Blow was good, but not as good.' "

---

[16] If you are interested in consulting services such as teambuilding, communication, leadership, etc., then please visit www.tompayne.com.

Julie asked, "But what if you had a horrific boss? Could you honestly say all of your bosses were good ones?"

"Yes I could. And that list would include Crazy Eddie.[17]

"I ever so fondly remember him taking me out on an all-night bender, telling me at 3 AM that we would have a breakfast meeting at 8 AM, only to have him sleep in and blow off this meeting that I happened to make. As for his behavior on the road, away from his wife…you don't want to know.

"Could I call Crazy Eddie a good boss? I sure could, can, and with a clear conscience. He actually taught me some valuable business lessons that I've used at other companies. As you can imagine, such a botch of a person had to have strong business skills to offset his personal liabilities.

"Would I ever want to work for Crazy Eddie again? Not in a million years. But that question is far different from whether or not he was a good boss.

"Just remember that these suicide invitations are fishing expeditions. With this question the hiring authority is trying to discover if you have problems with authority. If I answer this question by gleefully stomping on the memory of a nightmarish boss, the hiring authority might think, 'I wonder what he will say about me one day.' Or, 'It takes two to tango, so I wonder how he was a part of the problem.' Negativity hurts your cause, because negative expressions tends to cause negative responses."

Julie agreed. I then said, "Here is another invitation to down a bottle of sleeping pills,

'Describe your biggest failure in your last job?'

"If you were a tremendous success in your last job you may want to frame your answer as follows, 'That's a tough question. As my resume shows, I overachieved my objectives every year, sometimes by a large margin. So there weren't any big failures. But I did give a really lame speech at one of our award ceremonies and my guys hounded me about it for years.'

---

[17] Even the nicknames have been changed to protect the guilty.

"Humor can be used in interviews, particularly by someone who has made a positive emotional connection with the interviewer through stories, smiling, and demonstrating mastery over the interviewing process. When used at the appropriate time it can strengthen the emotional bond you are trying to forge.

"Or if you missed an objective one out of eight years you can answer, 'I'm proud of the fact that I made my objectives in seven out of eight years. These objectives were all stretch objectives that were never designed to be easy. So my biggest failure was missing my objective one year. It was also my biggest learning opportunity. It forced me to reconsider everything we were doing, from our training programs to our customer appreciation initiatives. And the changes we made throughout our organization resulted in me attaining my objectives every year after that.'

"Again, you start with a strength, you end with a strength and you transform your failure into a positive learning experience that made you better. Or, as the once popular cliché goes, 'It's all good.' "

Julie then asked, "How do you handle,

'Why were you fired from your last job?' "

"Depending on your actual experience, you could answer in one of the following ways:

> Our company went through many downsizings and I survived all of them except this one.

> Our company was bought and during the reorganization my position was eliminated.

> There were several political factions at work and my boss headed the one that lost. He and his team were let go.

> I was the last person hired in my department and was one of many who were then let go.

> I have a history of getting along well with my bosses. They are some of my strongest references. But for whatever reason, we just could not get along. This was very unusual and I am looking forward to enjoying a good work

relationship with my next boss.

My boss went through four CFOs in less than three years. So I look at my three years of employment as an achievement.

"The key to answering this question is to relate it to forces outside of your control, relate it to an issue that is in the past, or illustrate how it was an exception to the rule.

"Another question that begs the foolhardy to commit interviewing suicide is,

'What did you dislike about your last job?'

"My answer would focus on something that distracted me from producing results. For example, 'Paperwork would occasionally take time away from improving the quality of our products, reducing costs, and making my team stronger. However, some of the required paperwork was important, and audited by inspectors, so I always stayed on top of this. Though I'm not a great fan of paperwork, we passed every audit with flying colors.'

"Julie, I once had a job involving international travel. So I could truthfully answer, 'Expense reports. All of the currency calculations are a nightmare. Sometimes one report would take half a day to fill out.' In other words, every job has what can be called a 'crap-factor.' It has some necessary, but unpleasant task that is not directly linked to your success. Refer to them when answering this question."

"Oh No, Not That Question!"

"This part of the session may make you a little uncomfortable."

"This part of the session?" Julie asked sarcastically.

"Okay. This part of the session may increase your discomfort."

"Great. I can't wait. Bring it."

"Will do. Most people have one liability that makes them nervous. Every time it surfaces they freeze and their palms start to sweat. Do you have a liability like that Julie?"

"Yes, and I don't think even your Jedi mind tricks will help."

To which I replied, "Nonsense! Never think that way. If liabilities could never be overcome, we would all be without hope. So let's look this liability in the eye and address it with a technique that has worked well for me.

"Do you remember the story about my interviewing against someone who was far more qualified? I had been bouncing from one job to another and now had a huge liability, namely, a spotty work record.

"When the interviewer asked, 'Why have you changed jobs so often?' what could I say? Wasn't he simply stating an incontrovertible fact? Not quite. I responded with the ARTS technique.

A Is For Acknowledge

"The first thing you say is, 'I understand your concern.' That's it. I've acknowledged it, but I am not going to say another word in this acknowledgement phase, because I am determined to be like an iceberg, and my liabilities will remain beneath the surface. I immediately move to the next step of the ARTS process."

R Is For Redirect

"You redirect the discussion to something in your background that shows how you are capable of loyal employment: 'But I once worked for a company that lost half of its revenue in one year and was on the verge of declaring bankruptcy. They cut everyone's compensation...' The hook has been set. Now you test it."

T Is For Test

" 'If I was to show you how I not only stayed with them through these personally difficult times, but also turned this situation around would that allay your fears about me changing jobs too often?'

"The interviewer answers, 'Tell me more.' "

S Is For Story

"I then tell the story about my loyal tour of duty with a distressed company, 'Fair enough. I joined WOW, Inc., in 2000, and after being with them for six weeks their two best salespeople left and took with them half of the company's revenue. They had been planning this move long before I arrived. Compensation was slashed, travel expenses were cut, our prospects for survival looked grim.'

"If your story has a good hook it draws them into the narrative and by the end of the story they are impressed by the way you've answered their concern:

> So as you can see, under the worst circumstances, and for over a five-year period, I was not one to abandon ship. Through very difficult times I remained loyal, and my actions not only reversed this declining revenue trend, they restored the revenue we had lost.

"Your immediate past may generate questions that are best answered by performances further back in your career. The ARTS technique can turn a liability into an asset with a well-placed, well-written story.

"Would you be upset with me if I left the subject of suicide?"

Julie said, "Not one bit. But I'd like to know how many coaching clients you've lost during this session."

"Not one, so don't break my perfect record."

Showcase Questions

"All is not gloom and doom when it comes to questions. Other questions allow you to showcase your skills and achievements and we must be prepared for them. Often these questions allow you to use stories. One of them is,

'What have you learned from your mistakes?'

"You could answer,

> Mistakes have been my greatest teacher. When I first

became an accounting manager I had an extreme task-orientation. *Just get the job done* was my mindset. I focused on results to the point of forgetting there were people involved. So my style became too demanding. I intimidated others. I did get results, but they were costly. My team started to experience high turnover. So what did I do? I pushed harder and made things worse. Fortunately I had a great boss who saw the problem and worked with me to fix it. It involved how I communicate with others more than anything else. Because of his coaching, my leadership and teambuilding skills went from being liabilities to being strengths. My rookie mistakes led me to learning some of the most valuable lessons of my career.

"Put the mistake in the past and if you have a strong story that answers this question, then use it.

"Other showcase questions could be:

> 'What would your last supervisor say about you?'
> 'What was your greatest achievement?'
> 'What major challenges did you face and how did you handle them?'
> 'Describe your ideal boss?'

"Whenever you can, answer questions in a way that show how you confronted a challenge and overcame it. This does two things. It engages the interviewer's interest, because conflict is interesting. And it focuses your answers on providing solutions to problems they likely have. It shows how you could be a part of their problem-solving team. It sells without appearing to be sales-y. Stories are built around this premise of conquering a challenge, and the more traditional type of answer should have this conflict-resolution element when possible.

"For example, take this interviewing scenario:

> 'What would your last supervisor say about you?'
> 'I think he would say I was one of his most valuable players. Before I arrived he was having trouble making his revenue growth numbers. He made his sales plan in just two of the previous five years. But after I arrived he made

his sales plan four out of five years, and he publicly acknowledged this turnaround was largely due to my efforts.'

"This answer paints a picture of an obstacle and the jobseeker removing it.

"Liability questions, or suicide questions, deserve short, well-thought out answers that reveal as little as possible about your liabilities. Showcase questions, on the other hand, are best answered by stories or examples of overcoming obstacles.

"We're almost at the finish line. Are you ready to cross it?"

"Count me in," Julie said.

Lessons

1. Every liability should have a scripted answer that is memorized.

2. The ARTS technique is reserved for the truly difficult liabilities that you know you will be asked about.

3. Showcase questions are best answered by stories, or examples of overcoming obstacles.

11. Research, Your Questions, And the "Close"

The Open Opportunity

"Julie, when someone contacts you about an opportunity, ask questions like, 'Why is the opportunity open?'

"Did you ask this question when they contacted you about your new job opportunity?"

"No. The call caught me off guard."

"No problem. You can ask this at the end of the interview. But you need to ask it, because you want to know if the person before you was fired or promoted. Was a new territory added because of job growth? In other words, is this a great opportunity or a questionable one?

"If you are out of work, and have been for some time, then there is the temptation to take whatever becomes available. You are not in that position, but if you are later on, then remember that caution is always advisable. If you jump into an opportunity that lasts six months or a year, and you are fired because this company churns and burns through all of its employees, then you will have another resume liability to explain. Circumstances may make this opportunity an acceptable risk, but you should go into every new job with your eyes wide open. It may improve your survival rate.

"The second question you need to ask is, 'Can I have an updated job description?' This is something you need prior to the interview. So if you don't have it, then call their HR department and ask for it.

"Job descriptions should list your key responsibilities and accountabilities. It can tell you what skill sets the employer wants a new hire to possess. You can then develop stories and scripted answers showing how you've met these criteria."

"Thanks for the…"

Julie asked a question I had expected sometime before, "How do you remember all of that stuff? You've got ten stories, answers to liabilities and other expected questions, and now another ten answers to show how you can accomplish the job description's responsibilities."

"I remembered it because of the editing and rehearsal process. First, you write these things down and edit them several times. Then you rehearse them in your head. Then you read them aloud and time them to keep all answers below the two-minute threshold. This makes the answers and stories stick.

"Most people will never achieve perfect recall, but that is not the goal. The goal is to provide the gist of the rehearsed answers and to keep from rambling.

"Does that help?"

Julie said, "Basically, you need to work your butt off."

"Yes, but remember that this intense preparation is what enables you to relax during the interview. As the great Polish pianist, I. J. Paderewski, once noted about rehearsing, 'If I don't practice for one day, I know it; if I don't practice for two days, the critics know it; if I don't practice for three days, the audience knows it.'

"Even though he was a world-class talent, he still needed to rehearse daily. That said, on the day of the interview I may go over the material once and then focus on relaxing, projecting warmth and enjoying the interview."

"Be honest. You enjoyed interviewing? Seriously?"

"I did. The preparation's tough. It's like preparing for a marathon. The twenty-mile preparation runs are never very fun. The long tempo runs can be exhausting. But the day of the race is much better."

Research the Company

"Companies are not living things, but they develop a type of personality and culture. As best you can, learn their style. It will express itself in the way they contacted you about the job, and showed interest in you as a person. Did they offer you a job description, a contact person to call for answers to questions? Were they courteous, or did they make you feel like you were a bother?

"Their website will express a lot about their personality. It is like their professional photo for the world to see. Their vision and mission statement offers a window into their corporate 'soul.'

"If, for example, their annual report and their mission and vision statements focus on customer satisfaction, then you prepare customer-focused answers to potential questions. When asked about your strengths one of them might be the key customer relationships you developed and how these produced results.

"One of the purposes of researching a company is to determine if you fit their culture, or if your personality meshes with their corporate persona. For example, are they a cutthroat, take-no-prisoners type of company, and does this style suit yours? Fit is critical to long-term success.

"There's another important reason why you research a company thoroughly. If you don't, then you can't effectively answer, 'How much research did you do on our company?' Failure to answer this question can, by itself, destroy your chances. It suggests you are a person who isn't serious about this opportunity."

Julie said, "This question killed me early in my career. I thought I was interviewing fairly well. Then the interviewer said, 'I have one final question. How much research did you do on our company and this opportunity before you came here?'

"The truth was I hadn't done that much. So I answered, 'I reviewed your Annual Report,' and before I could get any further he said, 'Great. What did it tell you? What did you find out?'

"I said, 'It looks like you are growing nicely.' 'Indeed we are,' he said, 'but what did you discover about our CEO's vision for the company? Where does he want to take us?'

"I had to answer, 'I don't remember.'

"To which he replied, 'No problem. What else did you do for research?' I mumbled a few other lame responses and then a thought appeared in my mind, as clear as any thought I think I've ever had: 'Stick a fork in yourself; you're done.' "

"Some interviewers would make great Inquisitors."

"Yes, this guy was awful. We both knew the interview was over so now I became his cat's paw. He toyed with me for another ten minutes. He was a real creep, but now I never miss preparing for that question."

The Hiring Authority

I moved on to the next object of our research and said, "Through Google, LinkedIn, Facebook, and your own personal network, you will research the person who will be making the hiring decision. You want to discover potential connections you have with him.

- Where did he go to school? Was it a school similar to your own—was it a liberal arts college or one with a great reputation in engineering?

- Where has he worked prior to this job? In what positions?

- What does he like to do in his spare time? Golf, cook, garden, run?

"Then, when you first meet, you can make some small talk about a passion you both share:

"When I was researching your company I think I read somewhere that you love to cook. Is that right?"

"Wow! Your research is good. Yes, it is a passion I've had most of my adult life. Do you like to cook?"

"I do. I go crazy over recipes from the Mediterranean: Italy, Morocco, Spain, Lebanon, you name it. One of my favorite websites for recipes is Epicurious. Do you use it?"

"After a minute or two on this topic you can gently redirect it to the standard interview, because the mission has been accomplished. You might say, 'I didn't mean to get us sidetracked on cooking, but it is fun. You probably have a lot of other questions you would like to ask?'

"People see what they expect to see and what they *want* to see. You are trying to make a positive emotional connection with the hiring authority, because this can make him want you to succeed in your interview. A conversation about a shared avocation helps make this connection. So find out whatever information you can to help make this connection stronger."

Your Turn at Bat

"Eventually you get a chance to ask whatever questions you want. Be careful, because some questions, or failing to ask any questions, can make you appear desperate and ready to accept any job offer. Questions can also suggest you are a person who is discriminating and interested in managing her career.

"So whenever I am offered the chance to ask questions I focus on three things: The company's prospects, my fit and what they hoped to find in a new hire.

"The company's prospects are important, because I might be the last person hired before a downsizing. Last hired, first fired. If a company is growing, then the possibility of a downsizing is less.

"So find out what their competitive advantages are, because this has a bearing on their prospects. If they tell you, 'Competitive advantage? We are the largest, most established company in this industry,' then be careful. Dell, the computer maker, could have said the same thing before they tumbled. So could a host of other once-mighty companies. So check their current market share and what it was three or five years ago. Is their market share growing or declining?

"I also ask several questions about fit, because if I don't fit then I'll eventually quit, be fired, or be miserable. Some of the questions about fit are, 'How would you characterize your management style?' 'What's unique about your company's culture?' 'If people fail in this position, what is the number one reason why?'

"One of my final questions is, 'The interviewing process typically wants to make sure the candidate is a good fit. I also want to be sure. To help me determine this could you tell me what the most important qualifications of your ideal candidate are?'

"I'm trying to uncover information that will help me advance in this interviewing process. So if their answer is, 'We are a results-oriented company. We are looking for someone who consistently produces and who understands how important it is to generate good results, because that's why we're paying him.' I will then use this information in my final statement."

The "Close"

"As I've said, the traditional sales approach is all about closing. Ask for the order, or in this case, ask for the job. This approach makes no sense, because the decision-making team makes the hiring decision behind closed doors. So I don't try to close anyone, but I do ask to remain a part of the ongoing process.

"I'd typically say something like, 'You've just told me that you are looking for someone who is results-oriented. I think that's the ideal environment for me. Immediately after graduating, I joined the U.S. Army and it gave me a no-excuses mindset. Results were the only thing that mattered in the Army. I then applied this same attitude to every job thereafter. When you look at my track record, I've consistently produced results that grew revenue and favorably impacted the bottom line. I think this is a great opportunity and a great fit for me, and I'm very interested in pursuing this further. So I've got to ask, "Is there anything you've heard that might keep me from moving on to the next step in this hiring process?" If there are any concerns, I'd like to address them.'

"If he says, and he usually does, 'You've made a great impression on me, but once the decision-making team gets together we'll make a final slate of candidates and we will let you know, one way or the other.'

"Your last words can be remembered by the hiring authority because of the recency effect, so make them count. I would conclude by touching on the powerful emotion of pride by saying, 'The last thing I'd like to say is I've done extensive research on your company, and I've found you are considered to be the best managed, highest quality producer of nuts and bolts in the United States. You also have low turnover and high employee satisfaction, and I would be delighted to become part of your team. It was a pleasure to meet you and I hope we meet again soon.'

"If it is true, and everything you say should be true, then it is not false flattery and people want to hire people who want the job and appreciate the opportunity. So expressing this feeling is helpful.

"We just have a few finishing touches to apply and one of them is how technology is inserting some new and important style considerations into the interviewing process."

Lessons

1. Research the job, the company and the hiring authority before the interview. Be thorough.

2. Develop questions about the company's prospects, your fit and who would be their ideal candidate.

3. Express your strong interest in this opportunity and ask if you've failed to answer any objections that might prevent you from going to the next round.

4. Conclude by touching on the powerful emotion of pride.

12. Technological Twists

Julie discussed our interviewing sessions with her friends and they all had the same concern. Julie expressed it, "My friends are all asking me if your material is dated. They say, 'Technology is developing so quickly that whatever you've come up with must be out of touch with current reality.' What do you think about that?"

I'd heard this objection ten years ago, and knew it would become a constant refrain as the speed of technological change increased. This objection is easily answered.

I replied, "I think technology is inserting itself into the interviewing process in a way that we need to cover, but everything else I've taught you is based on human nature. When Gutenberg invented the printing press in the fifteenth century, human nature didn't change. When the Internet came on line, human nature didn't change. And when we decoded the human genome, guess what?"

"I'm guessing human nature didn't change."

"You got it. But technology does introduce some interesting twists that need to be addressed. Since style is still more important than substance, technology does confront us with some new style considerations."

Videoconferencing Interviews

"According to the Aberdeen Group only 10% of companies conducted Skype interviews in 2010. That percentage mushroomed in 2011 to 42%. So it's likely you will be Skype-interviewed one day.

"To prepare for a Skype interview, practice conducting one on the computer, and from the location, that you will be using during your interview. This will get you comfortable with the format and it will allow me to check out the lighting, your outfit, appearance and so on.

"Some things that you can't see will be obvious to someone else. For example:

- I can barely see your eyes because of the way the lighting has allowed shadows to appear.

- Or your forehead looks so bright and shiny it is distracting.

- The color of your blouse is too loud and distracting, as is its pattern. Solid colors, other than red, are better options.

- The background shouldn't be a large painting because all I want to do is look at the painting.

- Don't multi-task during this interview.

- No dog in the room. You don't want the interviewer to be jolted into another dimension by an unexpected, loud bark.

- Keep it out of the way, but a glass of water may come in handy if you develop a case of dry mouth.

- Keep a piece of paper and a pen nearby for taking notes.

- The great thing about Skype is it allows you to have post-it notes all over your computer to remind you about stories to tell and to smile. Please smile. A Skype interview is unnatural at first, and when we experience new things that are stressful we tend to be dead serious, emphasis on dead.

LinkedIn

"Finding a job is all about networking and LinkedIn is one of the most important job-related networks. It is a must for jobseekers. Recruiters, small businesses and large companies use LinkedIn to find employees.

"There are several ways to take advantage of this tool."

I then handed Julie a sheet detailing a few of the ways to make her LinkedIn presence more effective.

1. The headline for LinkedIn appears right below your name. It shouldn't be your current job title. Instead use this important piece of web real estate to tell everyone what it is you do. Instead of VP of Sales the 120 character headline could say, *Leader of Global Sales Initiatives, Developer of Effective Training Programs and Coach of Market Dominant Teams*. That uses up 111 characters and it has more punch than simply saying, VP of Sales.

2. When listing skill sets don't offer them in one continuous stream. Give each skill set an illustration of how you've used it. This is more effective than ten skill-sets clumped together.

3. Be giving. Do to others what you would have them do to you. Write unsolicited recommendations of others, because LinkedIn will then ask them if they want to return the favor. It is an effective way of gathering additional recommendations. If this fails to generate recommendations, then ask people you know if they will write one. And, to make it as easy as possible, provide them with a copy of what you want them to say.

4. One way to damage or limit your network is to try and connect with people you don't know. If five people report you to LinkedIn for attempting this, then you go on a blacklist and it will be much harder for you to expand your network.

5. Expanding your network can be helped by listing every

place you've worked or interned, because LinkedIn will then supply you with the names of all of the other people who've listed these companies. Then, if you know them, try connecting with them.

6. The LinkedIn browser tool bar is free and you should download it. If you go to job-hunting sites it can tell you how many people in your network work at the company you're researching.

7. Add common misspellings of your last name to the "Summary" field of your profile. Until you do this, someone who misspells your name may not find you.

8. LinkedIn has a limit of 50 groups. Join fifty groups, because this gives you access to all who are in these groups. It also gives recruiters, who are in these groups, access to your profile. Groups related to your skill sets, alumni, industrial, geography, or your interests are worth joining because your goal is to be seen.

9. Being seen is important, but so is seeing. The main menu bar has a jobs tab. Use its filters to check out what is available. Next, cash in the bonus you received for joining a group. Each group can have jobs posted that do not appear under the general heading. And if you drill down further, by clicking on job discussions, you will find additional opportunities that are not posted in the main group listing. These are micro-targeted opportunities.

10. LinkedIn also offers some excellent information about the companies you may be interested in, or interviewing with. This can provide you with information that changes your entire approach to the interview.

Twesumes

"Julie, what's a twesume?"

"You got me? A twit's resume?"

"Close. It's a 140-character, condensed, resume that can be broadcast on Twitter."

"A 140-character resume? You've got to be kidding. What's next? Haikus?"

"Maybe for a Japanese opportunity. But twesumes are taking advantage of a trend from corporate America. Companies are posting job opportunities via Twitter with links to take you to their career site.

"Twesumes are doing something similar. They have links to the jobseeker's resume, website and so on. Since 89% of companies used social networks to recruit people in 2011, it makes sense to stay with this curve, or ahead of it.

"Start by composing your twesume. Include in it: What you do, an accomplishment, a skill-set, your goal and a link to a more detailed profile. You can also add the hashtag: #twesume. You then tweet this twesume to your followers, direct message it to companies you are interested in, and even use this as your Twitter bio."

"I'm not sure this trend will have legs," Julie said, "but I love the way it doesn't seem like it will take a lot of work."

"Maybe not, but never underestimate the difficulty of making 140 characters powerful enough to generate a response.

"What you said brings up an important point. All of this technology-related stuff can get out-of-date quickly. Not too long ago LinkedIn was a small boutique app used by few. Now it's a mainstream app used by millions. So research the web during future job searches to find out what tech trends seem to be the most important at that time."

The Job Search Campaign

"Companies want people who can think outside of the box. So creative people are launching job search campaigns that include developing their brand on a website.

"These websites can have videos of the candidate, videos of people giving testimonials about their impact, and marketing campaigns that differentiate their product—themselves—from other candidates. You could post an interactive resume on this website with links to your blog, or to a position paper on teambuilding, or other important topics related to your field.

"One of the skills in the resume might be a link to a videotaped answer. For example, click on *problem solving* and the person with a job opportunity might be taken to a YouTube video that shows you telling a story about a problem you faced in a work situation and the way you solved it.

"There are endless ways to be creative about a job-search campaign, and this could open doors for you that will remain closed for others."

Lessons

1. Video interviews using Skype, or other services, are here to stay. Become familiar with the style issues that can create so much noise your message goes unheard.

2. LinkedIn is a powerhouse application that appears to be a permanent fixture in the job-search scene, but the way technology changes, this might not be true several years from now. However, its current scale and capabilities make it a useful job-search tool.

3. Twesumes: short, creative and—for now—worth the effort.

4. The job search campaign is about using creativity and technology to present your unique gifts and skills. Tying together a website, blog, YouTube videos, and an interactive resume, are ways of presenting yourself as a technologically savvy, out-of-the-box thinker.

13. Mock, Phone,
And Informational Interviews

Why Mock Interviews?

"Julie, I'm a big proponent of rehearsing for interviews and doing this on tape. How do you feel about that?"

"Not good."

"What is it about a mock interview that you dislike?"

"Try asking, 'What is it about a mock interview that I like?' The answer is *nothing*."

"Why?"

"I hate being put on the spot. It's unnatural and I don't think it helps."

"Okay, but here is why you need to love mock interviews. Training under stressful conditions prepares you for real-world stress. Videotaping a mock interview is a way of introducing stress to your rehearsing. It gets you used to answering questions under stressful conditions to help you handle the stress of an interview.

"One of the reasons why the U.S. Army's Ranger School deprives its students of food and sleep is to artificially create the stress that is all-too-real in live combat. So the artificial stress of a mock interview can be very beneficial.

"Rehearsing also develops what I call *interviewing responses*. To return to the military example, soldiers rehearse specific missions dozens of times because they may soon be operating in the most threatening and confusing environment there is: combat. These *trained responses* can help keep soldiers from completely freezing up when bullets are whizzing overhead and bombs are exploding around them.

"The interview is far less violent and threatening, but the same principle applies: *A person will perform in a chaotic and disorienting environment according to the way he has trained.* So if you want to take the fear out of the interviewing process, if you want to enjoy it, then make your excellence automatic. Rehearse, rehearse and then, after resting a while, rehearse again."

Safe, Effective Critiquing

Julie grimaced and asked, "So how does this painful process work?"

"Stop worrying about this being painful. It's not. It works the following way. I will ask you some questions that you will probably be faced with in an interview. For example, *tell me about yourself.* Your answer will be videotaped. Then we will watch it together.

"I will then ask you to critique your own performance by first telling me what you think you did well. Then you will tell me what you think you could improve on. Whatever you say you can improve on, I am not allowed to mention in my critique unless I disagree with you and think you are being too hard on yourself."

Julie looked confused, "Why start with me critiquing myself? You are the expert."

"For a couple of reasons. First and foremost, I want to create an environment where criticism is safe and accepted. It's easier to hear criticism from one's own mouth than from others. That's why you go first, and also why I don't repeat what I believe are your accurate criticisms. If you know what needs to be fixed, then why do I need to repeat it?

"When you are finished critiquing yourself, I will then tell you what you did well, and what else you can do better. Too often a critique makes it sound like the person did nothing right. That's why this approach always starts with praise.

"After the critique, you will rehearse what needs improving. I'll be watching and giving you feedback as needed. Once you feel good about it we will videotape you again and then critique this performance to see if you've improved, or if another session is required. If it still needs improvement, we will wait until tomorrow before trying again.

"How does that sound?"

"Not as terrible as I thought it would be."

Phone Interviews

I started the next subject with a question: "I know you don't like interviewing, but how about a phone interview?"

Julie cocked her head and said, "Seriously? If Dante had gone through a phone interview he would have added another level of hell to his *Inferno*. It would even be lower than the one reserved for people who drive slow in the fast lane."

"I think it's safe to say you don't like them, and I can understand why. Phones make what is already difficult even more so.

"We prepare for phone interviews virtually the same way we would for a regular interview. We research the company, the job description, and the interviewer. Preparing those tight, crisp answers is especially helpful. When someone drones on in person it is difficult, but someone droning on during a phone call is excruciating.

"A phone interview typically lasts 20-30 minutes. It may seem like forever, but that is not a lot of time. So don't save your best stuff for last. Your research should uncover two or three critical skills a person in this position must have. Have a brief story for each one of them. Telling three one-minute stories in 20-30 minutes is hardly overkill, and if you can make a phone interview more enjoyable, then you will separate yourself from the crowd.

"As with every other aspect of interviewing, style is crucial. They have to see you through your voice. So listen to how you sound over the phone. Call your own phone number and leave yourself a voice mail that is the answer to an interview question.

"Ask yourself, 'How does my voice make me look? Do I sound tired or energetic, warm or distant?' In other words, what emotions are evoked by my voice?

"If your voice sounds flat, then practice talking with a smile. Many people have used this technique to give their voice warmth. Standing while speaking can give your voice a tone of confidence and authority. Try it out. Record it and see if it works for you.

"I also recommend turning off call-waiting. Every phone system may be unique, but here is how I do it when I am being interviewed on the radio. When the producer calls, about 2 minutes before I go on the air, I ask, 'Would you mind staying on the line for about ten seconds while I switch off my call-waiting?' They happily oblige and I then press: flash, * 70, flash, flash.

"In your case, I would say to the interviewer, 'Before we get started, if you like, I can turn off the call waiting. It takes about 5-10 seconds.' He might say, 'No need to worry about that. Let's get started.' If they are okay with possibly being interrupted with beeps during the call, then that is their prerogative."

Julie asked, "What about having notes in front of you?"

"I highly recommend it, so long as you don't have to noisily shuffle paper. Unlike the Skype interview you can look down the entire time. So if you have a few pages of notes, then have them laid out in front of you. And along with these notes, a copy of your resume is a good idea. If they refer to it, seeing it might help you formulate a better answer.

"Sound-proof your interview. No music or TV in the background, and again, no dogs in the room."

"What have you got against dogs?" Julie baited.

"I love dogs and always have. But I need to make money to feed them, don't I? May I continue?"

"Please."

"Okay. Have a glass of water nearby in case your nerves give you dry mouth.

"And, as with all interviews, be prepared to ask questions. I'd particularly key in on *fit* questions, management style, culture, etc."

"So how do you communicate you are interested and want to remain part of this process?" Julie asked.

"I'd simply end the interview with my last prepared question. 'Based on the job description, my background, the company's culture and your management style, I think I'm a great fit for this position. That's one of the reasons why I am so interested in this opportunity. So I guess my final question is, is there anything preventing me from moving onto the next step in this process?'

"If they say, 'I have no concerns," you can add, 'Great. What's the next step?'

"He might then say, 'A final slate of candidates will be drawn up this afternoon and we will contact those candidates tomorrow.'

"I would conclude by saying, 'I hope to hear from you tomorrow and I've enjoyed speaking with you.' "

Julie said, "I know you said you liked interviewing, but can you honestly tell me you liked phone interviews?"

"Personally, I don't even like talking on the phone. But most phone conversations are not contests. When it comes to contests I prefer winning to losing. So I never thought of this as a phone interview. It was simply a different type of interview that required me to adjust my style."

Informational Interviews

I asked Julie, "What do you think about informational interviews?"

"I'm no good at them. Probably because I've only done a few of them," she answered.

"A structured approach makes them easier and effective."

"But why cover this now," Julie protested. "I'm going to be interviewed in a few days."

"Yes, and you will likely finish first. But there may come a time when you will need to look for another opportunity and informational interviewing will be a critical piece in your networking strategy. It helps you tap into the hidden job market, the opportunities that never get posted."

"Okay, I'm sold. Besides, it's always been a skill I wanted to learn."

"Smart girl. Let's get started.

"Most jobs are found through networking. Some put the percentage as high as 80-90%. So you develop a list of all of your networking contacts: Friends, colleagues from prior jobs, contacts from alumni and professional associations, people you know from church or other organizations, in other words, everybody.

"Your goal is to get three new contacts from each of these initial contacts. Do these people know anyone who is currently working and is a hiring authority? Those are the important contacts. And don't forget; when someone shares a new contact with you always ask him if you can reference his name. It can keep you from ending up in your new contact's spam folder."

Targeted Industries

"Hopefully these initial contacts will lead to hiring authorities who work within the industries you've targeted, because your goal is to develop a list of contacts within these targeted industries. If they fail to produce any of these leads, do not despair. You can add to your contact list by researching companies in these industries."

"Why limit it to targeted industries? Why not spread the net as wide as possible?" Julie asked.

"The purpose of an informational interview is, in part, to get information from someone in a specific industry to see if they think your skills are transferrable to their world. Certain industries are better fits for your skills, or are more interesting to you.

"Besides, by limiting it to a few industries you get to take advantage of the *small world* effect. People know people within these industrial small worlds and your networking has a better chance of making you visible within them. When you go after every industry at once it is harder to become a known quantity, or generate buzz about your candidacy.

"You will start by making a list of companies in your targeted industries. Then you will research them to develop a list of hiring authorities and their contact information.

Warm Calls

Julie said, "This is where the process gets hinky for me. I won't know these people and they won't know me. I don't want to cold call people I don't know. Why would they want to waste their time with someone who calls them from out of the blue?"

"Because you are not a problem seeking a solution, but a solution trying to learn about their problems so that you can solve them. This attitude alone will help warm up cold calls, and they need to be warmed up because cold calls typically fail.

"Do Google searches on these people. It could be they were just mentioned in a business article a few months ago. By referencing this article in your initial call you warm up the cold call.

"If you have any personal connection, it warms up the call. Did they once work in the same industry as you? Did they attend the same school, or a school in the same state? Do they have the same major? Are they members of one of your professional organizations? Did someone, anyone who knows him, refer you to him? By mentioning these tenuous connections the call goes from cold to warm.

"We'll cover what you would say in just a moment, but what is easy to forget is this: There is a hidden job market. The person I am speaking to may not have a position open for me, but he may know of someone in his industry who is looking. Or you may so wow him he thinks, 'We've always needed someone with these skills. Let's create a position.'

"There are other benefits gained from informational interviews. You get experience interviewing; you may learn of new ways to employ your skills that you never imagined; and you can expand your list of contacts."

Phases

"The first phase of the campaign involves you talking to anyone and everyone. The next phase may involve you speaking with people in targeted industries who occupy a job-level similar to your own, or who are one to two levels higher than you. Ultimately, you want to spend time with those who work at a level higher than yours, but your peer-group can offer valuable information. Since you are seeking a job that is either the same as theirs, or similar, they can help clarify whether or not your skill-sets fit the requirements of the job and the ways in which they do."

Securing the Interview

"The way to secure the informational interview can go through these steps:

1. Send an email or a message to this contact through LinkedIn.

2. Follow up with a phone call to ask for an informational interview.

3. Conduct the interview.

4. Express your thanks and gratitude.

5. Update them on your progress.

"So Julie, why do you want to keep them updated?"

Julie said, "When they do find out about a new opportunity I don't want to be the person they've forgotten about."

"Bingo!"

Julie said, "So far this process is looking easier than expected. Can you tell me what your email states and how you handle the follow-up phone call?"

The Initial Contact

"The first paragraph should read something like this:

> Hi Joseph,
>
> My name is Tom Payne and I received your name from Edward X, your counterpart at Acme, Inc. In managing my career transition, he recommended you as a helpful contact.

"You mention the referring person's name at the beginning of the email, and also in the subject line. It could read, *Subject: Referral from Edward X.*"

Value Statement

"The next paragraph is essentially your value statement. It gives a brief overview of where you've worked, some of your achievements and your skill sets. This should take about 30-60 seconds to read. So after you write it, read it with a stopwatch. Your smartphone has one."

Julie rolled her eyes and said, "I know that!"

"Of course you do. Anyway, this email should be able to fit on a single page and the value statement should take up the bulk of your message. Its purpose is to show how you are someone worth knowing.

"One difference to this value statement from others is the way you will want to make it broader in its appeal. You will be speaking to people in industries different than yours. So you will want to speak about how your achievements demonstrate problem solving, teamwork, and other areas that apply across businesses."

Request

The third and final paragraph requests the informational interview.

> To advance my career, I am looking to employ my talents in your field. To help make this transition I would like to benefit from your perspective through a brief, twenty-minute informational interview. To arrange a time I will call your office next week. I thank you in advance for your

consideration.

The Interview

Julie said, "This is seeming easier by the minute."

"And you know what, Julie? This process can actually be fun. Other people know what it's like to be out of work. Most will want to help. In some ways I found this process restored some of my shaken faith in humanity. It was encouraging to receive help from complete strangers."

Julie replied, "The task seems to be far more enjoyable once you've broken the code."

"Like so much else in life," I replied and then continued. "Once you secure the interview you will arrive in your appropriate attire armed with your best questions. You will thank him for his time and quickly offer your value statement. It can sound like this:

> Hi Joseph, thanks so much for your time. I'd like to start by offering a brief summary of my qualifications because they are directly tied into the questions I will be asking.

> I've worked for....

"Remember, you are a solution seeking problems, and the thrust of your value statement must make this clear. Because after your value statement you will ask questions that try to unearth problems that your skill sets can solve:

> What are the needs of an organization like yours? What are the problems you are trying to solve?

> How do you think skills like mine will benefit organizations like yours?

> What are the most important skills for succeeding in those positions I'm best suited for?

> How often do companies like yours hire from outside of the industry?

> What impact does the economy have on this occupation in good times and in bad?

Is this field growing?

"On line you can find resources offering 200 informational interviewing questions and you can pick and choose them according to what you think works best.

"The next step is showing how your skills can solve problems that are typical for their type of organization. This may lead them to eventually interview you for a position. But the important thing is illustrating the way you would provide organizations like theirs significant value, because this increases the likelihood he will do you a favor. Namely, give you some new contacts.

"Your next question is, 'Do you know of anyone in your field who I could contact to continue this transition process?'

"Whether he gives you additional contacts or not, thank him and ask one last question, 'Is there any way I can help you?'

"There are a couple of reasons why you offer your help, but first and foremost it is good to give and you have a lot to offer. From a purely psychological standpoint, it builds you up. You are not approaching people like a beggar waiting for a hand out. You are a professional whose skills can help an organization and a hiring authority, and you offer to help whether they reciprocate or not."

Questions?

Julie was an active listener. She would place herself in whatever scenario I defined. It enabled her to see where my advice was incomplete.

She asked, "Do I leave this person my resume?"

"Not unless they ask for it. This is not a pretext to conduct a job interview, or turn it into one. You've come under the auspices of an informational interview, so it needs to remain one."

"So should I bring a resume just in case she asks for one?"

"Yes. Always carry one with you, because if they ask for one it enables you to say, 'I always carry one in my briefcase, because you just never know.' "

"What if the interviewer loves you and keeps talking, and the interview now goes over twenty minutes. Do I cut her off or let it keep going?"

"A good rule of thumb is this. Most people schedule their work in 30-minute blocks. So if you go over 20 minutes that's okay. But I wouldn't let it go over 30 minutes unless this person was very, very insistent about keeping you there to learn more.

"Any more questions?"

"No. I like this format."

"I do to. It makes this informational interview a win-win for both parties."[18]

Lessons

1. Videotaped mock interviews offer an excellent coaching opportunity to improve performance.

2. Rehearsing in front of a camera adds pressure. This trains the jobseeker to deal with pressure during an interview.

3. Phone interviews are interviews minus the in-person contact. Treat them in much the same way as an interview with this exception: Check out how you sound over a phone and modify the way you speak as needed.

4. Informational interviews follow a format: Define your target audience, develop contacts in this industry(s), make the cold call warm, send an email followed by a phone call, and arrive at the interview with a scripted introduction and questions.

---

[18] Much of this material on informational interviewing comes from executive outplacement training I once received. This was supplemented by a seminar, given by Martin Gahbauer, at the Career Transitions Center of Chicago. His presentation can be found online at prezi.com. It is entitled, "Mastering the Art of Informational Interviewing."

Section Three:

End Game

14. Emotional Intelligence

I started this session with a question, "Are you familiar with the Emotional Quotient idea, or EQ?"

"Not really," Julie said, then added, "I've heard of it, but I'm not that familiar with the concept."

"It's a way of looking at human performance and it suggests our EQ is more important to achieving success than our IQ."

Julie said, "When I was a kid I only heard about IQ. No one talked about EQ. So why is this idea suddenly popular?"

"IQ failed to account for a troubling piece of data. Why did people with average intelligence outperform those with the highest IQs about 80% of the time? This suggested something other than IQ was at work when it came to performance."

"So what exactly is EQ?"

"It can mean different things to different researchers, but here is a definition that works for me. People with a high EQ are able to identify both their emotions and those of others. And they can control their emotions and behaviors to interact with others in the most effective way.

"There is an interesting difference between IQ and EQ. We appear to be born with our IQ. It doesn't change much over time. But we can grow our EQ dramatically. This effort is worthwhile because top performance and high EQs are strongly correlated."

"So what does it have to do with interviewing?" Julie asked.

"A great deal. I'm going to give you this brief outline of how to use your EQ during an interview. Read it if you have time before your impending interview, but first we need to rehearse your stories, value statement, and your scripted answers to questions."

"Is the video equipment ready?"

"Yes. Let's get started."

She put the following outline in her briefcase. What I handed Julie now follows.

Emotional Intelligence in Interviewing

Everyone prefers a communication style, and we are most comfortable with communication styles that are similar to our own. By recognizing an interviewer's style, and modifying ours to theirs, we can make an interviewer comfortable instead of irritated, and able to hear what we say instead of tuning us out.

So how do we discover the communication preferences of others, or our own for that matter? The Myers-Briggs Type Indicator® (MBTI®) is a tool providing these insights.

MBTI®: A Brief History

The starting point for this theory was the work of Carl Gustav Jung, a famous Swiss psychiatrist who studied under Sigmund Freud. He split with Freud and developed a different theory of personality based on types. Introverts and extraverts are two well-known types that his theory introduced to the world's vocabulary. They form a dichotomy, or a contrast of opposites, one of three he developed to explain the personality.

The mother-daughter team of Katherine Cook Briggs and Isabel

Briggs Myers added a fourth dichotomy; they also developed a self-reporting tool to help people discover their psychological type.

The Four Dichotomies

According to this theory there are four dichotomies and our preference for one category over another produces our four-letter type. These categories, and the associated letters, are:

1. Extraversion-Introversion, or E-I

2. Sensing-Intuition, or S-N (Intuition is represented by the letter "N," because the letter "I" was already taken by Introversion)

3. Thinking-Feeling, T-F

4. Judging-Perceiving, J-P (added by Myers-Briggs)

The following is an oversimplification of how our preferences produce a four-letter type. For example, an extravert (E), who gathers information through the senses (S), makes decisions logically (T), and prefers delaying the completion of tasks to the last minute (P), is an ESTP.

Throughout our lives we operate in all eight of the above categories, but we prefer to operate in one dichotomy-category over another. An extravert, for example, is capable of introverted activity, and engages in it throughout his life, but it is not his preferred mode of operation.

How does type affect interviewing success? We will start by looking at the fourth dichotomy—judging and perceiving—that is concerned with how we deal with the outside world.

(A brief aside: Some of the names for these dichotomies can be confusing. For example, if your preferred way of dealing with the outer world is through judging this doesn't mean you are judgmental. And if your preference is perceiving, then this doesn't mean you are more perceptive.)

Communication Preferences

How the judging type deals with the world is through imposing order on it. He is more scheduled, methodical and organized than the perceiving type, and prefers to drive things to closure rather than leave tasks undecided and open-ended. Finishing tasks energizes the judging type. He is almost never late for an appointment and is often early. He can grow impatient with people who take too long to get to the point. He is decisive and may make his hiring decision early in the process.

The perceiving type approaches the world in the opposite fashion. He is less structured, more spontaneous, adaptable, open-ended, and not concerned with rushing things to their desired end. He can be late for appointments and not be bothered by it, something unfathomable to many judging types.

But do not think perceivers are the ones who are always late and never finish a project on time. They can be every bit as effective at successfully finishing projects as the judging types, but they tend to do it at the last minute. Why? In part, because they want to gather as much new information as possible, since it may result in a better decision. But they also delay completing tasks because they are energized by the pressure of a deadline.

Frank Lloyd Wright and Perceiving

A classic example of a perceiver's response to the world and its demands comes from the famous architect, Frank Lloyd Wright. His iconic masterpiece, Fallingwater, was designed for Edgar Kaufmann, Sr., a wealthy Pittsburgh businessman. After nine months of waiting to see a drawing, Kaufmann called Wright one Sunday morning and told him he would be over before lunch to look at his drawings. There was one problem. Wright had yet to produce one.

How would he create a beautiful home that would perfectly fit into this property's stunning, unique topography in the two hours it would take Kaufmann to reach his studio? With nervous apprentices watching, and the results of a survey detailing the location of every boulder and tree on the property in his head, Wright began to draw. He finished designing his masterpiece in time for Kaufmann's impromptu visit.

No type is superior or inferior to its opposite. Every type has value. But can you see how one person's preferred style might drive another person with the opposite preference bonkers? Kaufmann had had it with Wright's delays and, in a true judger's fashion, drove the project to a successful conclusion.

Judging and Perceiving in an Interview

Now let's apply this knowledge to an interview. Let's say a judging type is interviewing a perceiving type. This particular perceiver is gregarious, loves the spotlight and answers questions at length. The judger has thirty question he wants to ask during his hour interview, and after thirty-minutes he has asked only seven. His frustration begins to mount with each successive "longwinded" answer.

To finish his interviewing task on time the judger starts to interrupt the perceiver's answers. The perceiver is visibly shaken by this and begins to withdraw. Finally, the judger, upon realizing there is no way he will ask all of his questions, begins to tune out what the perceiver is saying. He's had it with this failed interview. The perceiver's sterling qualifications no longer matter. He has disappeared along with his chances to secure this job.

Let's reverse this situation. The perceiver arrives late to his interview and asks the judger open-ended questions covering a broad range of topics. When he asks the judger about his favorite past time the judger says, "I love to learn. I read mostly non-fiction books that help me develop in personal and professional ways."

The perceiver then spends the next ten minutes exploring books he's read and how he's used them. He stays on this topic because he is gaining insights into the judger and discovering new books he might want to read. He's enjoying this spontaneous turn in this interview.

At first, this line of questioning seemed reasonable to the judger, but as it goes on for ten minutes he starts to feel uncomfortable and agitated. He begins to think, "What is the point of this?" Finally he interrupts the perceiver and says, "I know time is precious during our interview, and there is not much left. If you like I can send you a list of my favorite books and a synopsis of their impact on me. But before our time ends I would really like to give you an example of how I led my team from being mediocre performers into being a high-performance team."

The more assertive judger may think he is helping his cause by moving the conversation back toward his substantial achievements, but his communication style ensures a second place finish. The perceiver, who was enjoying himself, now thinks, "Do I really want a pushy, bullying subordinate who will probably try and tell me what to do?" The answer is, 'No!' "

Lesson One

The judgers prefer people to get to the point. Their mindset is, "I asked you what time it was. I didn't ask you to build me a clock." Endless jabbering can make them uncomfortable. They are typically more assertive than the perceiving type and will interrupt you to get to the point. Therefore, if you ramble you might annoy a judging interviewer. His thoughts may narrow to one: "When will this interview end!" As he tunes you out, your substantial achievements become moot. Sometimes an unsuccessful interview is due to our failing to modify our communication style.

We can recognize the judging type during an interview by their business-like approach. Not much time will be wasted on chitchat. They may say, "How was your trip to the office? Would you like something to drink?" And with that the pleasantries end and the interview begins. Finally, they tend to be more focused and intense in their appearance than most perceivers.

The perceiving types are more casual and relaxed in their appearance. They enjoy processing information. They will engage in chitchat because it may provide them with valuable clues about who is the best candidate for the job. Successful interviews will probably run over the allotted time. So relax and go with the flow.

You may think that my preference for concise answers will clash with this perceiving type, and to that I would say, "Wordiness obscures meaning and can make an interviewer struggle to understand you. This is not helpful. Keep your answers free of unnecessary verbiage and simply provide a perceiver with more, clear information." Stories are ideal for a perceiver and, as long as they get to the point, they are effective with judgers as well.

With this dichotomy we have a clear illustration of potential communication problems based on one's communication style.

Extraverts and Introverts

The extravert-introvert dichotomy is perhaps the most misunderstood. We tend to think of extraverts as the outgoing type who loves interacting with people while the introverts are shy, retiring wallflowers, but this view is inaccurate.

This dichotomy refers to the way these two types direct their energy and receive it. Extraverts direct their energy toward the external world of things and people. This means they have less energy available for the inner world of thought and contemplation. Introverts are the exact opposite. They direct their energy toward the inner world of thought and reflection and consequently have less energy for the outer world of people and things.

These types also *receive* energy from their external or internal orientations. An introvert can spend hours, or days, thinking about a problem that needs solving. They are energized by this activity, while an extravert would likely be drained by it unless they could talk it out with others.

Julie, to help you understand this dichotomy I am an introvert. Yes I was successful in sales, interacting with small and large groups for prolonged periods. I was also an infantry officer, one of the most extraverted jobs imaginable. So introverts will not always appear to be quiet and retiring. If their job requires the opposite behavior, then they will act out of type. But this is not their tendency or preference.

Lesson Two

Extraverts *tend* to be more expressive than introverts. They prefer interacting with others and the environment to being alone in the world of ideas and thoughts. They tend to speak faster and are more likely to interrupt. They are often more animated, action-oriented and sociable. They prefer to talk things out and this shows how even their thought process has an externalized, action-orientation.

These behaviors suggest the extraverted interviewer would not feel as comfortable with someone whose quieter behaviors suggested a low-energy level. Since people tend to judge others according to the gold standard of themselves, the extravert might wonder if the less expressive type has what it takes to get the job done. Therefore, it is wise to mirror, to a degree, the behavioral expression of the interviewer. But don't over do it or you will appear fake.

If the extraverted interviewer hijacks the interview and does most of the talking, don't be worried. Some extraverts feel most comfortable when they occupy center stage, and while they are performing favorable emotions are being generated. Smile as they perform—sometimes it is hard not to. Participate in their show when you have the opportunity. They will eventually get back to interviewing.

Unlike the extravert, introverts think things through before talking about them. So if you find your interviewer seems reserved, asks questions and quietly waits for answers, then know your clear, scripted answers will be well received, because introverts like clear concepts. Simply pause for a moment before delivering them. This would mirror the introvert's tendency to think before speaking.

If you have an extremely expressive personality, then toning down its wattage is a good idea. I know some extraverts who are so intense and expressive that they are overwhelming to other extraverts; so imagine how uncomfortable extremely extraverted behaviors can make some introverted interviewers feel. Would you hire someone who strums your nerves like a banjo string?

With both the introvert and the extravert the story format works well. Expressive, extraverted types love to tell stories and hear them. Introverts appreciate stories because of the way they can provide a clarifying context.

Objection

Some may feel this sort of behavior modification is verging on losing one's identity and becoming a fraud. They might feel uncomfortable expressing behaviors that are not natural. They also might fear their *playacting* that resulted in their being hired might later work against them when their new boss discovers their real personality and doesn't like it.

First, let's handle the objection of fraud. When a person is hard of hearing I raise my voice so they can hear me. I modify my behavior to be heard. Is that fraud? I normally don't speak with a booming voice, but the situation required it, and the other person appreciated my accommodating his communication needs. I am doing the same thing during an interview when I, for example, intentionally get to the point much faster than normal. If I fail to modify my behavior I risk being tuned out and not being heard.

As for a boss liking the modified me, who behaved in a way that put him at ease, but not liking the unmodified me I say: Isn't emotional intelligence understanding the impact of your actions on the emotions of others, and modifying them so as to produce the best results? So why would I stop modifying my behavior when it enables my boss to understand me and feel more comfortable around me?

Furthermore, why limit this modification to my boss? Why not use my emotional intelligence to behave in a way that is more satisfying to whomever I meet?

I won't change. I will still be an introvert who needs quiet breaks to be reenergized, but I also have the ability to function in the other type categories. I may never be as effective an extravert as an extravert, but I have functioned ably in an extraverted capacity on hundreds of occasions and will do so again.

Perception: Sensing and Intuition

Our approach to interviewing begins with behaviors, because they create perceptions that generate emotions that cause hiring decisions. The remaining four MBTI® categories are not as important when it comes to interviewing, because they are not as behavioral. They are mental functions that can produce behaviors, but they are primarily concerned with the internal world of gathering information (perception), and making decisions (judgment).

Jung believed there were two types of perception that formed our next dichotomy. The *sensing* type's perception of the world is based on sensory data. Our senses make us aware of things as they occur, and sensing types are focused on the here and now. Characteristics that often develop in sensing types are: practicality, attention to details, focus on the here and now, and so on.

The other category in this dichotomy is *intuition. Perception by the unconscious* was one way Jung characterized intuition. It produces hunches and the recognition of patterns that connect the dots in ways a sensing type might never see. Since patterns can extend into the unrealized future, intuitives are more future-oriented than the "enjoy the moment" sensing type. Intuitives are imaginative and creative. They trust their insights into people and patterns. Intuitives do not go 1, 2, 3, 4, 5 and therefore, 6. They go 1, 2, 3… 6.

Neither way of perceiving is superior to the other. Both are important and this is certainly true in the interview. The sensing-interviewing style might ask behavioral questions: "Give me an example of how you developed a marketing plan for product development? How did you test the plan? When the key products, based on your plan, were finally developed, how successful were they?"

The answers to questions like these should be specific, precise in their descriptions, and draw a clear picture of the steps you took. Sensing types may prefer behavioral questions, but it doesn't mean they aren't used by intuitives. I am an intuitive and I used behavioral questioning to confirm whether an interviewee possessed certain skill sets. Again, we prefer to operate in one half of the dichotomy, but we can and do operate in all eight categories.

Lesson Three

The most difficult preference to determine in others may be how they prefer to perceive, or gather information. Therefore, I do not recommend trying to determine the interviewer's perceptual preference.

Instead, follow this simple rule. If they ask for the specific behaviors you used to achieve certain goals, then provide specific behaviors. If they ask big-picture questions, then provide big-picture answers. This may sound obvious, but if your perceptual preference is intuition, then you are not as comfortable in the world of details as a sensing type and, true to your type, you may offer the big picture when the sensing type is wanting something far more specific.

Decision-Making: Thinking and Feeling

The decision-making dichotomy is named thinking and feeling. Jung did us no favors with these names, because thinkers have feelings and feelers can think. What makes thinkers and feelers different is the way they arrive at decisions.

A feeler's decisions are driven by how the decision impacts others. Their thought process is empathetic. They mentally place themselves into a situation in order to identify with those affected by their decision.

A feeler's values guides their decision-making. They also strive for harmony in their interactions with others.

Thinkers occupy the other end of this spectrum. They base their decisions on objective data. They can mentally withdraw from whatever situation confronts them in order to objectively assess the best path to take. They have a cause-effect approach to their decisions: "If this, then that."

While feelers avoid conflict, thinkers do not. Thinkers believe that everything can be made better so they critique things to improve them. During an interview they are likely to test someone to see just how much they know.

Lesson Four

If you are challenged during an interview, then the interviewer probably has a thinking preference. Answer his questions with logical statements regarding the value you offer. Cause-effect statements are well received by thinking types. "I did this and that, and it produced this result."

Feeling types will likely ask you about your impact on others. Answers illustrating how you helped a team or individual improve will resonate with this type.

Putting It All Together

We need to simplify this information or it becomes unmanageable. Therefore, during an interview, focus on the following type categories: Extraversion, introversion, judging and perceiving. They are more behavioral than the mental functions and they suggest ways we can modify our communication style. Recognize these types by their behaviors, detailed above, and respond accordingly.

The four mental functions are less behavioral; therefore, they have less influence on forming perceptions that generate emotions that cause hiring decisions. They should not be part of your interview preparation, unless you already possess an extensive knowledge of type theory.

Postscript

After Julie completed her first round of interviews she called me and said, "I think I nailed it! I used my stories, answered the suicide questions in a way that helped me, and my answer to 'tell me about yourself' did make the interviewer smile. And I can't believe it, but I actually enjoyed myself."

When she asked if there were any reasons why she should not be sent to the next round of interviews she was surprised to hear everyone say, "I've no objections. None. You did a great job. But I will need to meet with the others and discuss all of the candidates." These responses were far less guarded than previous interviewing experiences. They virtually said they wanted her to be a finalist. The next day they called to invite her to the final round of interviews.

Julie studied my notes on emotional intelligence and type and it changed how she answered questions during the interview. She felt the hiring authority was a judging type because he started and ended on time and was always to the point. If her analysis was correct, then Julie's crisp answers were music to his ears. The HR director, on the other hand, appeared to be a perceiver. She was much chattier, casual and relaxed. Julie modified her style by using all of her stories during the HR interview, and adding some details to them. To her succinct answers she added casual asides.

She could not tell if her interviewers were introverted or extraverted, so she simply mirrored their behavior to a degree. With an interviewer who was animated she was slightly more animated than usual, and none of the other interviewers appeared to be reserved or living in the world of concepts and ideas.

The hiring authority challenged her during her interview, on more than one occasion, and this suggested he was a thinker. So I cautioned Julie, "If you've gotten his type right, then understand he will be thorough. Don't lose your composure if this next interview is tougher than the first."

It was a tougher interview, but Julie was more than up to the challenge, and she increased the distance between her and her remaining competitor for this opportunity. She was beaming when she called me after the interviews.

Once again, I cautioned her, "Don't get too high or too low. This interviewing process is not over. But when it is over, win or lose, the outcome is due to your actions. And even if you do lose, I hope you sense your improvement as an interviewee."

"If I lose?" Julie asked. "If that happens I will be both amazed and a little sad. But I'm no longer afraid. Their response to my new style is 180 degrees different from what I've experienced in the past. And I know—you don't have to tell me—it's because I'm running in the right direction."

She got the job offer one day after her final interview. I then covered one last detail: negotiating the best deal possible.

15. Negotiation

Julie Victorious!

Julie finished first. Everyone else failed to medal in this pitiless, job-interviewing contest. Prior to receiving the phone call extending the offer, I coached Julie on how to accept the offer. It involved her thanking them, expressing her excitement about the opportunity and asking them for five days to think about the offer.

When they asked if something was wrong she was also coached to say, "Oh no. Nothing's wrong. It's just that this decision is so important. It could literally change the course of my career. So I just need some time to get over my excitement, think about what you've offered me and come up with an appropriate response."

The HR person said, "Okay. Then we look forward to hearing from you on," she checked her calendar, "Monday."

As I told Julie, the request for extra time accomplishes several things, but foremost among them may be this: With each passing day all of the other candidates become less viable choices should she have difficulty coming to an agreement. This would strengthen her negotiating position.

After she hung up the phone she said, "I got it!"

"You sure did." I glanced at her notes and added, "And what you got was an excellent offer."

"I know. It's more than I expected and a good bit more than I used to make. Shouldn't I accept it? If I ask for more, doesn't that run the risk of angering them and having them pull their offer?"

"Julie, where do you come up with this stuff? Put yourself in their shoes and think. They want you. They made that clear during the interviews, and their offer makes it even clearer. They're not offering you this much because they are afraid you'll ask for more. They are making their rich offer because people in this position make this much, and because they think you're worth it and want you on board.

"Now they've gone through five of the best potential candidates for this position. Do you really think they want to walk away from you so they can call number two, the one they just passed over, to see if he is still interested after a week has passed? Is desperate ever as desirable as worthy?"

"Okay," she said, "but I don't want to blow it when I am so close."

"Neither do they. Nor do I, for that matter. Do you remember how you resisted me when I said, 'Tell them you will be back to them in five days with your answer'?"

"Yes. But their response still makes me a little nervous. They sounded concerned."

"They are. Concerned about possibly losing you. They don't know if you are interviewing with another company and are waiting for this competitor to make a better offer.

"Another reason why you never accept an offer immediately is because of the way it can send a bad message."

"How?"

Negotiating Psychology

"It has to do with negotiating psychology. If you've ever thrown someone a low-ball offer on, for example, a used car, and the seller immediately accepted your offer, then are you jumping up and down for joy over your good fortune?

"I doubt it. The chances are two thoughts are troubling you.

Thought one: Heck! I know I could have done better.

Thought two: Something must be wrong with this car.

"So we should never immediately accept the first offer a hiring company makes. They may wonder if you are as good as they thought you were, because it appears you value yourself less highly than they do.

"What you are running into is your own mindset. You formed a picture in your head of what they might offer you and then their actual offer was much higher. Their offer is overwhelming you. These mindsets affect all sorts of negotiations, like yours. But you need to destroy this mindset and replace it with reality.

"Reality is this: You ran in the right direction and appeared to be heads and tails better than your competition who kept running in the wrong direction. You came across as not only more competent, but also as more likable. They *want* someone like you on their team. So stop being surprised by the strength of their offer."

The Warning

"I was once solemnly told by a recruiter the following, 'The person who interviewed before you was offered the job. But he asked for money and they pulled the offer. You can do whatever you want to do, but if you want this job, then I wouldn't ask for more money.'

"I quickly placed her tip into my 'Bizarre Advice' file and prepared to negotiate for not just a little more money, but for a lot more—25% more on the base salary, a signing bonus, and another week of vacation.

"The end result was this: I got everything I asked for. Negotiating for a better package is almost never wrong, unless one's negotiating style is."

"The *style* issue resurfaces," Julie said. But this time she was not fighting the concept that style is more important than substance during the interviewing process, because she had witnessed this principle in action.

Asking for More

"So Julie, how much more would you like to get through your negotiation prowess?"

"I don't know. Would a $15,000 bump on the salary line be excessive?"

"I don't think so, but it depends somewhat on what the offer amount was and what the typical salary range of your positions is."

"They offered $170,000, as you know, and the range is typically in the $160 to $220 range. It depends on seniority, the magnitude of the responsibilities, and other stuff."

"So what is your counter?"

"My counteroffer requests a salary of $185,000, or a $15,000 raise, and... what else?"

"Before the what else, we need to adjust what you are asking for. If you want a $15,000 raise, then you need to ask for $30,000."

"What? You've got to be kidding me!"

"No, I'm once again more serious than a heart attack. If you want to get an $185,000 salary, then you need to ask for a raise that takes you to $200,000. This is called the bracketing principle. The mid-point between their offer and your counteroffer is $185,000. So if they came back with a counteroffer that was $5,000 lower than what you sought, or $180,000, then what would your counter be?"

"$190,000, or $5,000 higher."

"Exactly. You make a counteroffer so that the mid-point ends up at $185,000, or where you want to land."

"But what if they accept my proposal of $30,000?"

I smiled and said, "Now that would be a bad problem to have, wouldn't it? That's what happened to me when I proposed a 25% increase. They gave it all.

"But the counteroffer shouldn't stop at an additional salary request. Ask for an additional week or two of vacation. And ask for a

$15,000 signing bonus. These signing bonuses are one of the easiest things to get, because CFOs understand how this is a one-time, non-recurring charge. They are so used to dealing with bigger issues, that these small, non-recurring expenses are almost never nixed."

"That sounds great, but what if the size of my request angers them? What if it leads to a contentious negotiation that gets me started on the wrong foot?"

"Remember how you used mindsets to your advantage in the interview?"

"Yes."

"Well we'll use that quirky process in these negotiations."

The Win-Win Negotiator

"I like to make counteroffers by email. It gives them something in writing to analyze. Sometimes what you say over the phone to create the mindset that you are a fair and flexible negotiator is overshadowed by the emotional impact of your request for much more money. And since what you said isn't in writing for them to review, your mindset may never get set, so to speak.

"An email also keeps the hiring authority from being placed in the uncomfortable position of having to respond while trying to get over the shock of your counteroffer. With an email, he can review your offer, calm down, re-read the message you are communicating, and then respond.

"The mindset I want to create is of a fair, flexible negotiator who believes the final offer can be a win-win. And just like the other mindsets I've created, this one is the truth.

"Here's how you do it. You begin your email with the following."

I then read:

> I was very excited to receive your offer. You will find my counteroffer below. Since we have never negotiated with each other I would like to introduce my approach to you. I aim for a win-win solution in every negotiation. I am

always open to discussing and modifying my counteroffer(s) because I know we can find a creative, mutually agreeable solution.

"The purpose of this intro is to remove fear. I've heard some career coaches say, 'This is unnecessary. They know that.' But I say, 'How could they know this if we've never negotiated before? Since some people are unreasonable negotiators, then why not address this fear up front?'

"I want them to know that I am not the type to draw a line in the sand. If the counteroffer has to be modified in their favor, then I'm open to that."

"Then what comes next, the substance of the counter?" Julie asked.

I replied, "No, the style of the counter."

"I should have known."

"The email continues."

I read:

I am countering your offer of a $170,000 with a request for $200,000. I will be happy to discuss, at length, how I think we can make this work for both of us. There are many creative options available that I'm confident would satisfy us both.

I am countering your offer of two weeks of vacation with a request for four. I had three weeks of vacation in my past two positions and believe that four will help me maintain my hardworking productivity throughout the year, year after year.

Finally, I am requesting a $15,000 signing bonus. This will benefit both of us because it will enable me to invest in advanced workshops and other things to make me more productive.

I look forward to discussing this counteroffer with you and making it work for both of us.

I looked up from the email and said, "It is likely you will only get one week of extra vacation, but you may get two. Again, that would be a nice problem to have. And they may come back with a salary increase that takes you immediately to $185,000. If that happens, what's your counter?"

"Counter? I accept it. Don't you agree?"

"I do. They've made a strong counter that takes you to where they believe you want to be. They aren't playing games. I interpret this action to mean they want to end the negotiation by letting you achieve your negotiating goals. So going back with a counter of $192,500 would have a poor risk-reward relationship. It may result in you getting a small bump in additional salary at the cost of bad feelings."

Unexpected Gyrations

I then addressed some what-ifs: "Let's say you've made your counteroffer and they call you up to discuss your email. The first words out of the hiring authority's mouth are, 'Your counter is a lot more than we have budgeted for this position. It's a deal breaker. It's too high.'

"The worst thing you could do is argue that it isn't too high, because this would turn the negotiation into a confrontation. Instead, follow the feel-felt-flexible-find formula. Its purpose is to neutralize negative emotions and reinforce the mindset that you are the ultimate win-win negotiator.

"You say the following:

> I understand how you *feel*. Many hiring authorities have *felt* the exact same way. But first I want you to know that I am a *flexible*, reasonable person, and nothing in this counteroffer is set in stone. And once we look at my counter in a different light, I think you'll *find* it's a win-win. Since this position doesn't have the budget for it, perhaps we can change the position slightly by giving it additional responsibilities. I could handle the following extra duties: X, X, and X. And that should more than justify my counteroffer.

"Now first off, I don't think they will come back that strongly against your counteroffer, but if they do, and you make such a non-threatening, firm and intelligent response, then this negotiation should add to your already strong reputation."

"Okay. But what if he comes back and says, 'Julie, I'm sorry I have to tell you that we cannot change the position and we do not have the money budgeted for this position to meet your additional salary request.'

"What do I say then?"

"I would say, 'I understand. And I don't want this negotiation to take up much more of your valuable time. So can you meet me half way and bump the salary up to $185,000. Will that be within the budget?'

"It could be the person you are dealing with is unfamiliar with negotiating and you need to help him reach the right conclusions. And if that is still more than is budgeted for this position, then I'd ask, 'What is the amount you've budgeted?'

"If they tell you a number that is $10,000 over the offer, then ask them, 'Is your counter-offer now $180,000?' You ask this question because you can't assume things when it comes to money discussions. We need to hear it from his lips and then see it in writing.

"If he says, 'Yes it is. You drive a hard bargain.' And if the other negotiating items were resolved, you could reply, 'I gladly accept your offer and now these negotiating skills will be put to use for you.' Then ask for an emailed and fed-exed copy of the adjusted offer letter.

"But let me make this clear, I'm just responding to your hypothetical questions. I can't imagine their initial offer is that close to the top salary they have budgeted for this position."

"One last question. What if they had $10,000 worth of room left and refused to offer it?"

"That would be a major red flag. When a company is completely inflexible about negotiating a pay increase to a new employee who they are trying to woo, then imagine how slim your chances are of receiving a raise once you get on board. So be careful about joining a company that is inflexible during the negotiation phase. Let this understanding guide you: If they treat you poorly on the front end, you will be treated much worse on the back end.

"There are exceptions to this. A retained recruiter may have marketed himself to the hiring company as being able to make the negotiation process smooth and seamless. One of these guys once asked me, 'If the company were to make the following offer would it be acceptable?'

"If I said, 'Yes,' then how would I be able to come back and ask for more? It was a clever ploy, but since I wasn't born yesterday I replied, 'I have no doubt whatsoever that we will be able to come to a mutually satisfactory agreement.' Then, once the formal offer was made, I upset his apple cart with a higher salary request and more. He didn't like this, but he wasn't the one who was going to be paid for my years of hard work."

The Hiring Authority's Response

When the hiring authority received the counteroffer he was initially stunned. He wanted to hire Julie, and still did, but did not want to seem like a pushover in these negotiations. He went to his boss and said, "I can't believe she's asking for so much more. My offer was a huge bump in pay for her."

His boss reviewed her emailed counteroffer and said, "Yes, but she's not demanding this counter. So let's consider it. The salary we offered her is at the low end of the range, isn't it?"

"Yes, but it's much more than she was making."

"I got that. All we are doing here is figuring out how we respond to her counter. Okay?"

"Sure."

His boss continued, "Now she was the best candidate, right?"

"Yes, by a wide margin."

"I'm betting you would have been willing to pay more than

$170,000 for some of the less-qualified people you interviewed, right?"

"Yes, but their current salary, or last salary, was higher."

"I don't think that's the issue. The issue is, 'Is she worth all or some of what she's asking for?' When we hire someone we want to get the best talent we can afford. So let's look at this in a slightly different way. You wouldn't be happier paying more for a less-talented person, would you?"

"I get your point. I'm fine with paying her more. I guess I just didn't want to seem like a pushover to you or to her. So what's my counter to her?"

"Give her what she wants on the vacation and signing bonus and half of the increase she's looking for on her salary."

"Wow! Why so generous."

"I don't know. I think it's because I like her style."

Negotiation Concluded

Julie could not believe their counter-offer.

I told her, "I'm happy for you Julie."

She accepted the offer and now my work with her was almost finished. We would meet just two more times. The summary of those meetings is the subject of the concluding chapter.

Lessons

1. Never accept an initial offer immediately.

2. Negotiations are rarely problematic when you establish the mindset that you are a fair and flexible negotiator who always aims for a win-win.

3. When negotiating a higher salary learn what the range is and use the principle of bracketing.

4. When confronted about your counter-offer, use the feel-felt-flexible-find formula.

5. A company's unwillingness to budge an inch during a negotiation is a red flag that should not be shrugged off.

16: Simplify. Focus. Achieve.

Julie was still experiencing a high. She felt like she had been stumbling around in the dark for a long time and then someone, who owed her nothing, handed her a flashlight. Suddenly the interviewing process made sense. She also found her lost mojo, increased her confidence and her income.

I had taken her through the Myers-Briggs self-assessment and helped her confirm her best-fit type. She was amazed at how the tool helped her understand the way she was psychologically wired. Based on this information she was now developing a plan to leverage her strengths and minimize her weaknesses. In short, this consultation delivered a lot more than she bargained for.

"How much do I owe you for this?" she asked.

"For what?"

"For all the help you've given me. I wasn't even going to ask for a signing bonus until you told me I must. I almost feel like I should split it with you."

"Almost? I wanted to talk to you about that, because I want it all."

Julie looked concerned and said, "Please tell me you're kidding."

"I am. You are paid in full. I was just doing a favor for a friend." I smiled and joked, "Besides, you couldn't afford me."

"I don't doubt that. But can I make one final request?"

"Sure."

"You probably have a pretty good handle on who I am and where I am, so do you have any advice on what I should focus on to improve myself?"

"That's a complex question," I said, and then added, "I'll have to think about it and get back to you."

A day later we met away from the office at a bakery that made a great cup of coffee. I thought it would be a nice place to say goodbye. After getting a cup of coffee and sitting down I asked, "Do you remember when I introduced you to the concept of radical responsibility and no excuses?"

She smiled and sarcastically replied, "One of the greatest days of my life."

"I'm sure it was. Anyway, radical responsibility is an idea I recommended you follow because it leads to better results.

"I have another idea that might be helpful. We're going to cover the process I used to understand and master the art of interviewing. It's a three-step problem-solving process.

"Are you ready?"

"You know the answer," Julie smirked.

Simplify

"Yes I do. Okay, the first step is to simplify.

"Here is what this means in practice. When we are confronted by a complex problem we must simplify it, or reduce it to its core issue, because until we do we don't understand it. Its complexity overwhelms us. We see its hundreds of issues and all them vie for our attention, like a classroom full of squirming kids, each raising their hands. Pick me! Pick me!

"At this stage the problem is just confusing noise, and unless we simplify it we won't even be able to speak about it intelligently. For example, whenever I read a book that is impenetrably complex my first thought is, 'The author doesn't understand his subject. He cannot make his complex subject simple to others because it is not yet simple to him.'

"Complex problems are like tiny, chaotic weather systems. They never move in straight, predictable lines. They seem random and illogical," I paused, then added, "until we study them from 100 different angles, from up close and far away, for extended periods of time and then again after taking a break.

"Over time, these hundreds of variables within the problem begin to reveal their connections and a picture starts to form. Various patterns emerge and then suddenly it appears, the single pattern that explains the problem's essence. This pattern, image or idea, is like the key that cracks a code.

"With this key we can now address the problem, because we understand its essence, its driving force. But until we understand this we will address whichever peripheral issue shouts the loudest, or hits us the hardest, and the core problem will still exist, waiting to ambush us somewhere down the road."

Microsoft: A Case Study

"Now let's look at how this idea worked at Microsoft, the software giant that still rules the PC world.

"While Bill Gates was CEO he did something few people take time to do.[19] He thought deeply. And not just for a few hours, or for a day. No, he went on week-long retreats, twice a year, to some secluded spot where he could study the problems, threats and opportunities facing Microsoft. These sessions were called *think weeks*.

"During a think week, in April 1995, he was able to see how a game-changing pattern had emerged: the Internet. The Internet was still a baby at that time. Netcraft, an organization that tabulates the

---

[19] Bill Gates was a co-founder of Microsoft Corp. He was its CEO until 2000 when he voluntarily stepped down as CEO to let Steve Ballmer run the company. He assumed the role of chief software architect and then left the company in 2008 to work on his philanthropic foundation.

number of websites in the world, announced its first tally a few months after this think week. According to them, there were only 18,000 websites at that time. To put this in perspective, in the year 2012 over 50,000,000 new websites appeared.

"So the Internet was small, but it was beginning to grow fast, and Gates saw a pattern emerging from the chaos of data he was trying to understand. He expressed his vision in an internal memo that was circulated in May 1995. It was entitled *The Internet Tidal Wave*. The title alone communicated the following urgent message: If Microsoft doesn't get in front of this wave the company could be washed away.

"But for our purpose the key point is this. He was faced with hundreds of threats and opportunities, but he was able to reduce this complexity to one unifying idea: the Internet. The complex had become simple and he now grasped what was truly important.

"The pattern that makes a problem understandable also suggests the problem's solution. The Internet became popular after Netscape's web browser made the World Wide Web accessible and useful. In this struggle to be a dominant player in the Internet space, Gates thought Microsoft needed to win the browser battle and they did.

"Gates then handed the reins of the company over to Steve Ballmer in 2000. Shortly thereafter, in 2002, their web browser, Microsoft Explorer, topped out at a whopping 96% share of the web's usage."

"Wow! I never knew they were once that dominant."

Enter Steve Ballmer

"Yes, 96% is an amazing stat. And I'm glad you used the past tense, because Explorer is now a distant second place behind Google's Chrome web browser. That's obviously a bad stumble, but nothing like the failure to see the emerging importance of *mobile computing*. I'm going to read something from today's Wall Street Journal. It shows how Ballmer either missed this pattern, or failed to understand its importance:

Months before **Apple** Inc. unveiled its iPad in January

2010, the tech world was buzzing about mockups of a tablet computer from **Microsoft** Corp. Created by an inventor of the company's Xbox videogame machine, the Courier folded like a book and let users sketch and jot ideas on a touchscreen.

That spring, Microsoft Chief Executive Steve Ballmer told employees at Courier's Seattle laboratory that he was pulling the plug on the device.[20]

"As the article goes on to say, more than 200 million tablets will be sold in 2013 and only a tiny percentage will run Windows. Since tablets are replacing PCs for many people, Ballmer's inability to look at the chaotic complexity of their changing world, and see where it might be headed, might one day result in Microsoft becoming another Kodak. But, since he has announced his retirement, to the market's thunderous applause, that outcome is unlikely."

"You really don't like this guy, do you?"

"I don't know the man. But in fairness to him, Microsoft's revenue has more than tripled during his fourteen year reign as CEO. So, he obviously hasn't been a total failure. But this isn't about Steve Ballmer. It's about problem solving. That's what this model can help you with."

Julie lifted up a mock glass and said, "To Ballmer! We barely knew ye."

"Arrrgh!" I replied, in my bad imitation of a pirate, as I lifted my mock glass. Then I got back on topic, "Until we see the threat and opportunity clearly, how can we possibly respond to it? Complexity confronts us with hundreds of potential courses of action, and all of them may be bad. After all, the only good course might be hidden in the complexity of the problem. For this reason, understanding our problem to the point where it is simple, and can be simply expressed, is crucial.

---

[20] "Next CEO's Job: Fix Microsoft Culture," *Wall Street Journal,* 26 August 2013, sec. B, p. 1.

"Are you following me?"

Julie said, "Yes. After all, it's simple."

"Julie, you never let up, do you?"

"I am an acquired taste. Hang with me long enough and you'll love me."

All Ideas Are Tested and Welcome

"I'll have to trust you on that one, and that provides the segue to the next critical step. When it comes to the ideas we have, and the patterns we think we are beginning to see, we must doubt them. They must be distrusted and ruthlessly critiqued. Why? Because we've seen how false assumptions, which are based on unsound ideas, are misleading. So, we need to be guided by a fundamental distrust of everything but that which is true, that which stands up to analysis and real-world testing.

"However, just as we distrust and test every potential solution until it is proven, we welcome every new idea. And this is due to a fundamental shortcoming everyone seems to share. We seem to be wired to want to go in the wrong direction, in many cases. There is a fork in the road and we find ourselves drawn to the wrong path. So many things seem counter-intuitive to us. Didn't we experience that in the world of interviewing?"

"Yes," Julie recalled, "I used to believe the hiring decision was rational, and substance was more important than style. The wrong path always seemed to be the right one."

"This sort of phenomenon happens more times than we think, or would care to admit. It tells us that we need to distrust ourselves or, to put it in a way that may be easier to accept, we need to be humble. When someone offers a solution that is the exact opposite of what we believe to be true, we need to think, 'I've got to check this out, even if it ends up proving me wrong.'

"What we are trying to develop is the ability to simplify the complex by disproving all possibilities that are false, and not by excluding points of view that differ from our own.

"Our beloved Mr. Ballmer now makes a return appearance." I

continued to read from the Wall Street Journal article:

> During a meeting with Microsoft employees in 2005, one worker brought up how Apple had reshaped the ways people bought and listened to music. He asked Mr. Ballmer whether Microsoft should try to compete with iTunes.

> Mr. Ballmer asked the room for a show of hands. "How many people think Microsoft is in the business of selling music?" he said sarcastically, according to a former company product manager in attendance. No one raised a hand. More than a year after the meeting, Microsoft launched its own digital-music player, the Zune, but it never caught up to Apple's iPod.[21]

"The question is not, 'Who thinks Microsoft is in the music business?' it's, 'Should it be?' But by sarcastically bullying a subordinate into silence, a valuable viewpoint that was starting to see an emerging pattern was lost. No, its worse than that. Ballmer's flamethrower shut down the entire room. Who dared to speak after that? Then, when they finally saw the importance of this idea and launched the Zune, they failed in the second phase of this process by not focusing."

Focus

"During the simplify-phase we concentrate our minds on *understanding* the problem. But the second phase focuses on *actually solving* it, or *implementing* the solution. We move from effective thinking to effective doing.

"The simplify-phase is trying to discover what is essential or truly important, and the focus-phase responds to this by dedicating all of our available time and resources to achieve this important end. Because, after all, where else is our time better spent?

"Once Gates saw the threat and opportunity of the Internet he focused Microsoft's enormous resources on beating Netscape in the browser war. Without this single-minded focus he may not have succeeded. Netscape had about an 80% usage share of the

---

[21] "Next CEO's Job: Fix Microsoft's Culture," sec. B, p. 2.

global browser market, so taking over from such a dominant force was not going to be easy.

"The browser war that began in 1995 went into 1998 with Netscape still holding a commanding lead. It took the development of over four versions of Explorer, and over three years of focused effort, for Microsoft to finally achieve its goal of browser dominance.

"The Zune needed the same focus if it hoped to achieve parity with the iPod, or to even become a respectable second choice in the market place. Instead, after a few iterations, they killed the project.

"Once you've determined something to be essential to your success, you commit your resources to attaining this objective. Just like you did to your interview prep. I'm betting you spent many an hour working on this while we were apart."

"More hours than I would like to admit to."

"And when we studied the problem from many angles did we not see a simple pattern emerge?"

"Yes. I think it's called running in the wrong direction. I was basically doing everything the wrong way."

"But once you understood the problem it became fixable. You then focused and you achieved."

Achieve

"You're going to love this," I said with a smile.

"Why does that always mean I am actually going to hate it?" Julie responded. "I figured you were laying in the weeds, preparing some parting shot."

"No, nothing that dramatic. It's just that when we achieve something significant, as you just have, it reveals another potential problem you may face, or anyone who achieves something may face."

"Great. Bring it."

"Here it comes. Because of the way many of us are wired we allow the following to happen. After we succeed, we immediately start looking for another important problem to solve.

"Does that sound like you?"

"Yes, and I'm guessing that suit also fits you quite nicely."

"Yes. It's tailored, fitted and worn on a near-daily basis," I confessed. "But we need to resist this temptation to move from intense work to intense work, unless the situation is truly dire. That's because it takes a great deal of effort to produce a big win, and you need to positively reinforce this by celebrating and resting. Rest, in many ways, is the goal. And it is for reasons that are, as you would expect, counter-intuitive.

"Are you buying this?"

"No. It makes no sense. But I'm listening with an open mind, because I've grown humbler over the last few days."

"Humble is good. Anyway, I like to use running as a metaphor for this part of the process. When a runner goes out on a training run, let's say it's speed work, he is breaking down muscle tissue. That is what the exertion-side of the training equation does. It breaks down. Now if he does speed work every day of the week, for weeks on end, he will soon end up lame, because he is only breaking down muscle tissue and not building it back up. Building our muscle tissue back up requires the rest-side of the training equation. Because it is during rest when this broken-down tissue is repaired and made even stronger. That's how training works.

"You would think rest would make us weaker, but we actually grow stronger through rest. It's one of the many counter-intuitive curve balls life throws at us. So, take time off. Use some vacation time to pursue whatever it is you love to do in your spare time, and rest your mind. There are spiritual ways of resting that help you grow stronger—prayer, meditation, and so on—but I also find it important to engage in mindless pursuits. Read a thriller or a romance novel or whatever you prefer. Just make sure it's about 50 IQ points south of Faulkner and James Joyce. Watch movies that require you to leave your brain at home.

"Then, some time in the not too distant future, you might be surprised at the insights that come to you, unbidden. The dots are being subconsciously connected. T.S. Eliot wrote his most famous poem, *The Waste Land*, while he was at a sanatorium taking what was called a *rest* cure. He had a vision of the current culture and developed a style of expression that changed the poetical landscape. Rest made him stronger."

"I bet you that idea goes over well with clients you consult with," Julie said with smiling sarcasm.

"Some get it, some don't. But its not that we work less. When we're at work we work. But when we rest we focus on resting. And we celebrate our wins by doing something special.

"Take right now, for example. You've just won big in your interviewing and negotiating. What have you done to celebrate? Or, the more interesting question, how do you celebrate?"

"I've done nothing to celebrate, but when I do," she paused to think a moment, "I sometimes treat myself to a spa day. You know, a Swedish massage, facial, mani-pedi… girly stuff."

"When was the last time you treated yourself to a spa day?"

She thought for a while, "I can't even remember."

"Then call your favorite spa and book a full-day appointment for the first available opening. Okay?"

"Yes boss," Julie answered as she saluted.

"Good. Here is what I know will be your favorite part of our time together. My final words."

She was uncharacteristically silent before I continued, "So long as you follow this path your life will be a quest that never ends. It will be a succession of achievements, and it will also give you an unexpected gift. You will never live in a rut. Each problem now requires you to approach it according to its own unique terms."

Until Then…

I then took us toward the inevitable parting of ways. "Julie, I've really enjoyed working with you and getting to know you."

Julie looked down and was a little upset over saying goodbye. We had been through a lot together in a compressed period. When I first met her she was emotionally raw, lacking in confidence and confused by what was happening to her in job interviews. Then, by showing her how her situation was far from hopeless I helped her stand up. By showing her the right direction I was able to turn her around. And by coaching her I'd gotten her to run in the right direction.

Her voice quavered a little as she said, "I don't know how to thank you. You've been a big help."

"Your thanks are payment enough. In a few months, let me know how your new situation is working out."

She smiled, gave me a hug and said, "Will do." Then she walked out the door to continue her quest that has yet to end.

Appendix: Do I Need Career Assistance?

If you are seeking a job, then the answer to the above question is, "Yes, you need career assistance." The only time this answer might be, "No," is when there are no low-cost options available, and all other options are beyond your budget. The good news is there are several low-cost options.

The Lowest-Cost Option

Free. How's that for low cost. Where do you get free career assistance? Many churches, particularly the larger ones, offer a variety of free services, or they will charge a minimal fee to cover the materials used and tests offered. For example, Willow Creek Church, in the northwestern suburbs of Chicago, is one of the largest churches in the country, and it offers a variety of services to jobseekers. The same applies to some synagogues. So check out what your house of worship offers.

The career services department of your college may offer life-long career development services. This can include being plugged into a career advisory network wherein alums offer you advice and answer questions to help you in your job search.

Ask your local Chamber of Commerce about whether or not they will be offering career/job fairs in the future. Many of them do.

The Low-Cost Option

The Career Transitions Center (CTC) of Chicago offers three months of assistance for $200 for members of a sponsoring institution (go to www.ctcchicago.org for a list of these sponsoring institutions), and $300 for those who aren't members.

The CTC offers a wide range of programs to assist jobseekers, but the resource most jobseekers rave about is the coaching. When I went through a very expensive executive-outplacement program, attended by CEOs and the like, I was coached and it was vital to my improvement. However, the CTC offers more coaching than I received for a fraction of the cost. In their program you get to meet a coach once per week for three months (or twelve 40-60 minute sessions) as part of your $200/$300 payment. Were it not for the contributions of around forty volunteer coaches this service could never be offered for anything close to this price.

I also serve as one of their volunteer coaches, but signing up for this course does not guarantee I will be able to work with you. The coaching assignments are made based on the choice of the student and the availability of the coach. Once the coach's slots are filled, and they can be filled weeks in advance, he or she is, for that time period, unavailable.

Most of you reading this are not living in the Chicago area, but I imagine most cities offer some form of career assistance at a reasonable price.[22] Research them and take advantage of them if you can afford to do so. A benefit of many career-assistance programs is the way they enable fellow jobseekers to connect. These contacts can offer valuable emotional support as the weeks of searching become months. If you've been able to search alongside others you will be in a much better place—mentally and emotionally—when an opportunity appears out of nowhere.

---

[22] Please send me (tom@tompayne.com) information regarding **not-for-profit** programs in your city. This information on the CTC of Chicago gives you an idea of the value these programs can offer.